SHOO THE NOISES

Shoo the Noises

RECLAIM YOUR FOCUS AND MANIFEST YOUR DREAM LIFE

ANAMIKA MISHRA

BLOOMSBURY
NEW DELHI • LONDON • OXFORD • NEW YORK • SYDNEY

BLOOMSBURY INDIA
Bloomsbury Publishing India Pvt. Ltd
Second Floor, LSC Building No. 4, DDA Complex, Pocket C – 6 & 7,
Vasant Kunj, New Delhi, 110070

BLOOMSBURY, BLOOMSBURY INDIA and the Diana logo
are trademarks of Bloomsbury Publishing Plc

First published in India 2025

Copyright © Anamika Mishra, 2025

Anamika Mishra has asserted her right under the
Indian Copyright Act to be identified as the Author of this work

All rights reserved. No part of this publication may be: i) reproduced or transmitted in any form, electronic or mechanical, including photocopying, recording or by means of any information storage or retrieval system without prior permission in writing from the publishers; or ii) used or reproduced in any way for the training, development or operation of artificial intelligence (AI) technologies, including generative AI technologies. The rights holders expressly reserve this publication from the text and data mining exception as per Article 4(3) of the Digital Single Market Directive (EU) 2019/790

ISBN: PB: 978-93-61315-07-7; eBook: 978-93-61311-49-9
2 4 6 8 10 9 7 5 3 1

Typeset in Adobe Garamond Pro by Manipal Technologies Limited
Printed and bound in India by Gopsons Papers Pvt. Ltd., Noida

To find out more about our authors and books visit www.bloomsbury.com
and sign up for our newsletters

To my beloved parents, whose love transcends time, space and beyond. You were, you are and you will always be with me, within me. I love you both. This one's for you!

Contents

Preface and Acknowledgements ... ix

1. As Noisy as It Gets ... 1
2. Been There, Done That ... 3
3. The Cost of Noises ... 7
4. Your Brain: A Servant or a Master ... 11
5. Too Many Forms of Success ... 16
6. Identify Your Noise ... 23
7. Heal Emotional Wounds ... 50
8. Rewire Your Brain for Optimism ... 62
9. Cultivate a Resilient Mindset ... 86
10. Power of Self-Belief ... 96
11. Build a Supportive Network ... 101
12. Boundaries to Protect Yourself ... 104
13. Mindfulness ... 117
14. The Perfect Balance: Mind, Body and Soul ... 142
15. Your Greatest Noise: Your Comfort Zone ... 146
16. Self-Worth and Acceptance ... 150
17. The Science of Habits ... 156
18. Manifest ... 169
19. Embrace the Noise-Free Life ... 186

About the Author ... 190

Preface and Acknowledgements

BEFORE YOU BEGIN READING this book, I want you to know that regardless of where you are right now or what state of mind you are in – whether you have experienced failure or success – I am always rooting for your growth.

Shoo the Noises is a collection of insights drawn from my personal experiences and learnings, interwoven with stories and quotes that have inspired me. More than that, it is a practical guide designed to help you shoo away the noises in your life, elevate your overall well-being and manifest your goals.

You are free to read this book at your own pace. Every moment you invest in it will add meaningful value to your life. Even if some concepts feel familiar, take them as gentle reminders to bring you back on track and help you stay aligned with your goals.

Heartfelt gratitude to my publisher, Bloomsbury, for being such a wonderful team. Your support and belief in this book have made this journey even more special.

Together we all rise!

1

As Noisy as It Gets

LIFE CAN OFTEN FEEL like a noisy place.

Imagine being in a crowded room where everyone is talking, making it hard to hear your own thoughts. This noise comes from different directions – from the expectations others have of us, from doubts we have about ourselves, and from the reality that things do not always go as planned.

Picture this: you are in a big, bustling city, surrounded by all kinds of sounds – cars honking, people talking, machines whirring. Life is a little like that – lots of things happening at once – and it can get overwhelming. The pressure to fit in, meet other people's expectations and conform to a certain image can cloud and clutter our thoughts.

In this noisy place, there is also a voice that sometimes says, 'Can I really do this?' It is like having a best friend who doubts you. Maybe you want to try something new, like learning a skill or starting a project, but that sceptical voice whispers, 'What if I am not good enough? What if I fail?' That inner critic is what we call self-doubt, and it can be one of the loudest noises we face.

Then there are moments that feel like a thunderstorm. Losing someone important or going through a difficult breakup can amplify that noise, making it seem even louder. These setbacks and challenging times make the noise in our lives even louder. It is like trying to find peace in the middle of a storm.

On top of all this, there are everyday challenges, such as doing well in school, getting along with friends or dealing with responsibilities. It is like a constant buzz of things we need to handle. Imagine trying to read your favourite book or watch a movie in a room full of people talking loudly. That is what these everyday challenges can feel like.

And just when we muster the courage to shoo away the noises within, another challenge arises. It is like stepping onto a busy street where everyone is telling you, 'You cannot do this. It is too hard,' or thinking, 'What if they laugh at us?' This external noise – the opinions and doubts of others – might tell us that our dreams are too big or that we are not capable. This noise can be discouraging and make us question ourselves.

Noise in your life is every blockage, barrier or obstacle that hinders your growth. It encompasses every thought, action or behaviour that obstructs your path to elevation. This applies not only to your career, dreams and goals but also to your personal life, like your well-being, relationships and duties.

But here is the catch: life does not come with a mute button. We cannot make the noise disappear. Instead, we must learn to navigate through it. It is like putting on noise-cancelling headphones to focus on what truly matter to us.

I wrote this book to help you find those mental noise-cancelling headphones that will enable you to focus on what you want from your life. Although I learned this a little late, I firmly believe it is better late than never. We must learn to manage the noises within and around us while confronting our doubts, facing tough moments and tackling everyday challenges.

Life can be noisy, but amid all that noise, we can discover our own tune. Let us embark on this journey together to learn how to shoo away the noises that try to drown out the melody of our lives and succeed in all aspects of life.

2

Been There, Done That

When I was a child, the idea of writing a book felt like an impossible dream. One major reason was that I believed my English language skills were not good enough. Although my skills were not lacking, I let external noise affect my self-confidence.

I attended an English-medium school in Kanpur, an industrial hub in northern India, which was regarded as one of the best schools in the city.

I was appointed class captain every year, winning all the debate and declamation house competitions and scoring A+ grades in all subjects. I was also the vice-captain of my school sports team and actively participated in and won dance and drama competitions. However, a small incident shook my confidence and made me doubt my abilities.

Our school had organised an inter-class story-writing competition where my house teacher selected another student's story over mine. When I asked for the reason, she replied, 'Oh, look at the beautiful words she has used and how beautifully she has framed the sentences! Your story is good, but it is straightforward and to the point. It did not entice me.'

I was heartbroken and it made me doubt my abilities as a writer. I could not help but think that maybe she was right – I could not write well.

In the next grade, I had to read *David Copperfield* by Charles Dickens as part of my coursework. After finishing the book, I felt a renewed determination to pursue my dream of becoming a writer, no matter what.

However, the thought of telling someone I wanted to write a book filled me with fear. What if people laughed at me? What if they pointed out all the mistakes I made? My English teacher had said my story did not captivate her. How could I possibly write stories?

These worries made me doubt my abilities. A small rejection from a story-writing competition lingered in my mind for a year and a half, convincing me that I did not belong in the world of writers. My dream of becoming a writer seemed out of reach.

One day, I mustered the courage to share my dream with the person closest to my heart – my mother. She was not only a homemaker, a wife and a mother but also a writer who crafted enchanting fairy tales for children.

Hesitant yet hopeful, I shared my dream of becoming a writer with my mother. I braced myself for questions or concerns; instead, she listened with a warm smile. It turned out that she had faced similar doubts when she started her journey as a writer.

In her gentle, wise way, my mother said, 'Self-doubt and fear are just noise that everyone encounters.' She recounted her own struggles and victories, emphasising that these noises are hurdles we can overcome. 'We must shoo away these noises,' she advised, 'because self-doubt is our biggest enemy.'

My mother's advice became my guiding light. She told me, 'Beta, fears and doubts are like the dirt on a tube light, blocking it from illuminating the room. Once we brush away this dirt, the brightness of our dreams can shine through.' This insight resonated deeply with me and completely changed my life.

It is often said that the lessons and experiences we have during our early years leave a lasting impression on our lives. It was my mother who helped me understand that being a writer is not solely about having flawless English or using complex vocabulary that makes a reader rush to google the meaning. Writing is about telling stories, sharing ideas, inspiring people and connecting with them through words. English is merely a language – a tool of communication. I began to realise that my unique perspective and experiences were important, and they could contribute to creating something meaningful.

After talking to my mother, I began writing and submitted my first article for my school magazine. I was surprised when my article was selected and published in the annual school magazine. I was in seventh grade. This experience boosted my confidence.

I started writing regularly – composing short stories, poetry, articles and essays. I was still learning; I was not perfect and made mistakes, but I did not let that stop me. I found joy in expressing myself, even if my writing was not flawless. I learned that improvement comes with practice and that everyone starts somewhere.

Every self-made billionaire was once a crying baby, and every grand mansion started as a blueprint. It does not matter where you are today; what truly matters is where you will reach tomorrow.

As I continued to write for my school magazine and later started my blog in 2007, my confidence grew. I realised that my voice, with all its imperfections, was my strength. People appreciated what I wrote.

I discovered that individuals value authenticity and genuine stories. I learned that the fear of not being good enough is merely a hurdle, not a roadblock.

Your fears do not define your ability to reach great heights. My insecurities did not determine my journey to becoming who I am today – an author, travel blogger and life coach.

If you are passionate about something, do not let self-doubt hold you back. Your voice matters, and your story deserves to be told, regardless of how you express it.

With my mother's encouragement, I began to actively shoo away the noises that held me back. I realised that whenever I felt inadequate, it was just a noise trying to drown out my aspirations. Whether it was the fear of making mistakes or worrying about what others might think, I learned to confront these noises head-on.

Through my journey of pursuing my passion for writing, I learned that much of the fear we experience is often of our own creation.

Shooing away noises is not just about silencing the world around us; it is also about conquering the uncertainties within ourselves.

Today, as I follow my path as a writer, I carry this wisdom with me. It serves as a reminder that while our fears may be loud, with courage and determination, we can silence them and allow our true aspirations to resonate even more powerfully.

This wisdom is not exclusive to the realm of writing.

Every person, regardless of their aspirations or dreams, grapples with their own set of noises in various aspects of life. Whether chasing a dream job, starting a business or venturing into something unconventional, the noise of self-doubt can be deafening. Fears surrounding failure, unmet expectations or choosing the wrong path can resonate loudly. Relationships – whether romantic, familial or friendships – also come with their own set of fears. Concerns about rejection, inadequacy or anxiety about an unknown future can create discord in our hearts.

Financial worries, too, add to the set of fears. The fear of scarcity, the stress of financial instability, concerns about making the right investments or even earning less than your friends and relatives can be overwhelming.

The universal truth is that everyone encounters their own unique set of fears, which can obscure their path to success. While these fears are not the same for everyone, the process of shooing them away shares common ground.

We just need to remind ourselves that the noises of all sorts can be shooed away.

Ask yourself the following questions before proceeding to the next chapter:

- What is your professional dream or goal?

  _____

- What is your dream or goal for your personal life?

  _____

3

The Cost of Noises

WE OFTEN TAKE THE presence of noises for granted, but the cost we pay is greater than one can ever imagine. Often, people do not realise how much these noises obstruct their paths.

These noises can be both subtle and overt, and they can pull our focus away from our goals. They can be so detrimental that sometimes people even give up on their goals.

Productivity and Quality

When we allow noises to interfere with our work or goals, our productivity suffers. We may find ourselves spending more time on tasks than necessary or in some cases, we may fail to complete them altogether. Noises, whether internal or external, pose a significant challenge to productivity by disrupting concentration, impairing focus and increasing stress levels.

These noises fragment our attention, leading to decreased efficiency and effectiveness in completing tasks. Moreover, they can elevate stress levels, further compromising productivity by hindering cognitive function and decision-making abilities, resulting in poorer outcomes.

Noises can significantly compromise the quality of our work. When we are not fully focused, we are more likely to make mistakes, overlook important details or produce subpar outcomes.

Misjudgement

Noises can cloud our judgement and impair our ability to make wise decisions. These noises can make it difficult for us to think clearly and make informed choices. Sometimes, we might rush into decisions without properly considering the consequences or overlook important factors before making a choice. Things like past hurts, criticism from others and even time spent on social media can distort our thoughts, making it challenging to make good choices. It is like having fog in front of our eyes, which makes everything appear blurry and difficult to see, potentially leading us to make decisions we may later regret.

Delays

Noises often contribute to procrastination and delays. Instead of tackling important tasks directly, we may find ourselves procrastinating or postponing them in favour of more immediately gratifying activities.

The most common form of noise that makes us delay our plans is the pursuit of perfection. We often think that we are not ready, believe we need to learn more, think we need to make improvements before starting a project or wait for the perfect time to begin.

A close friend of mine is a brilliant dancer. He has been planning to start a dance tutorial channel and open a dance studio for a long time. When I ask him why he has not started yet, he says he needs to reduce his belly fat and lose weight before he begins. He is talented, good-looking and has everything it takes to start a dance page. I even shared examples of famous dancers who weigh more than he does, but he still feels he is not ready. How did this doubt and insecurity enter his mind? This is because his relatives and friends constantly comment on his physical features, reminding him how handsome he used to look and insisting he needs to lose his belly fat, thus slowly chipping away at his self-esteem.

His situation is not unique; I have many mentees who feel they are not good enough and worry that if they take a step forward, people will laugh at them and judge them.

This and many other forms of noise are dangerous. They make us delay things. We do not realise that every individual is capable of achieving anything they wish. Another important thing we should keep in mind is that we should not care what people think. Why? Because people do not pay our bills, they do not put food on our table and they will not come when we are alone, overwhelmed with stress. People will gossip and point out mistakes regardless of what we do.

Mental Well-Being

Imagine you are trying to focus on something important, like studying for a test or finishing a project. But every few minutes, your phone buzzes with notifications, your siblings start arguing loudly nearby and you keep thinking about all the things you need to do later. These are noises and they can interfere with your mind.

When you have noises in and around you, they can make you feel stressed and overwhelmed. It is like your brain is constantly switching gears, trying to pay attention to too many things at once. This can leave you feeling exhausted and frazzled, making it difficult to find a moment of peace.

Noises also disrupt our ability to concentrate and think clearly. Instead of focusing on the task at hand, your mind keeps wandering off to other thoughts. This can make it harder to remember things, solve problems and perform at your best.

Over time, dealing with all these distractions can take a toll on your mental health. You might start feeling anxious or even depressed because you are always on edge, trying to juggle everything at once. It is like your brain never gets a chance to relax and recharge.

These noises can take a huge toll on our mental health and emotional well-being, leading to feelings of dissatisfaction and a sense of unfulfillment, which may result in mental illnesses such as depression and paranoia.

Does that sound scary to you?

But this is not the end. Every single brain on this earth is different, so the way these noises affect each person can vary greatly. We cannot predict the damage these noises may cause or are already causing in our lives.

When I lost both my parents within a span of one and a half years, I fell into depression. It was a trauma that fundamentally changed my life. Despite being a certified life coach and healer, I still struggled to regain my former pace of life. I decided to quit writing. I wanted to abandon everything.

It is important to identify your noise and have a clear understanding of its impact. Later in the book, I have shared how I overcame the biggest noise of my life. For now, I just want you to ask yourself three questions and write the answers below or in your journal.

- What is your biggest fear regarding your dreams and goals?
  _____

- What was the last thing you tried and failed at, and then did not try again?
  _____

- If you were given a magical power to accomplish one goal in your life right now, what would that goal be?
  _____

4

Your Brain: A Servant or a Master

WE HUMANS GENERATE APPROXIMATELY 60,000 thoughts every single day. Of those, approximately 75 per cent or around 45,000 are repetitive. These repetitive thoughts can greatly impact our lives.

Think of them as little architects quietly shaping the blueprint of our destiny. When we continuously think the same thoughts over and over again, they begin to influence our beliefs, attitudes and behaviour.

Imagine you have recurring thoughts like 'I am not good enough' or 'I will never succeed'. If you keep replaying these thoughts like a broken record, they begin to sink in and become part of your reality. They can hold you back from taking risks, pursuing your dreams or even feeling happy and fulfilled.

The good news is that once we become aware of these repetitive thoughts, aka the noises, we have the power to change and shoo them away. We can challenge those negative beliefs and replace them with positive ones, ultimately reshaping the course of our lives.

It is like being the director of your own mental movie. You get to choose which thoughts make it onto the big screen and which ones get left on the cutting-room floor.

Your brain is a powerful tool, capable of shaping your thoughts, emotions and actions in profound ways. It holds the key to unlocking your potential and achieving success in life. By combining psychological insights with logical reasoning, the brain enables you to co-create your destiny and navigate the journey toward your goals.

At its core, the brain is the control centre of our entire being. It processes information, generates thoughts and regulates our emotions and behaviours. Through its intricate network of neurons and neurotransmitters, the brain handles the complex interplay between our thoughts, feelings and actions.

One important psychological principle that illustrates the brain's role in shaping our destiny is the concept of neuroplasticity. Neuroplasticity refers to the brain's remarkable ability to reorganise itself in response to new experiences and learning. This means we have the capacity to shape and strengthen neural connections through deliberate practice and positive reinforcement.

For example, imagine someone who aspires to become a skilled musician. Through consistent practice and dedication, their brain undergoes changes that enhance their musical abilities. As they continue to hone their craft, the neural pathways associated with musical proficiency become more robust, ultimately contributing to their success as a musician.

As I mentioned earlier, the brain plays a crucial role in shaping our beliefs, attitudes and perceptions of the world around us. Cognitive psychologists have demonstrated that our thoughts and beliefs influence our behaviour and decision-making processes. This phenomenon, known as cognitive bias, can either propel us towards success or hinder our progress, depending on the nature of our beliefs.

Consider the example of someone who harbours noises such as self-limiting beliefs about their abilities. These beliefs may stem from past experiences or negative feedback received from others. As a result, their brain processes information in a way that reinforces these beliefs, creating a self-perpetuating cycle of doubt and insecurity.

Conversely, individuals who cultivate a growth mindset – believing in their ability to develop and improve through effort and perseverance – tend to face challenges with resilience and optimism.

Their brain actively seeks out opportunities for growth and learning, paving the way for greater success and fulfilment in life.

The brain's capacity for problem-solving, creativity and innovation enables us to adapt to changing circumstances and overcome obstacles along the way.

We need to understand that what we allow inside our brain shapes our reality.

Naturally, our brain is biased towards negative thoughts. For instance, if someone tells you that you look beautiful or handsome today, you may feel happy for a few minutes, a few hours or even a day. But that positive feeling will fade away. However, if someone says you are ugly and that they do not like you, this negative comment can trouble you for weeks, months or even years.

This is only because our brain is biased towards negative thoughts, similar to forming a good habit and a bad habit. If you or someone you know struggles with a bad habit or addiction, such as excessive alcohol consumption or smoking, you may have noticed that it was easy for the person to develop these habits but difficult to quit them.

This is not your fault. Throughout human evolution, our ancestors needed to be hyper-aware of potential threats and dangers in their environment to survive. As a result, the human brain developed a 'negativity bias', prioritising negative information over positive information. This bias helped our ancestors avoid dangers like predators, poisonous plants and other risks. Therefore, negative thoughts tend to capture our attention more easily because our brains are wired to be sensitive to potential threats.

Negative emotions, such as fear, anger or sadness, often evoke stronger physiological and emotional responses than positive emotions like joy or contentment. This heightened emotional intensity associated with negative thoughts can make them feel more powerful and overwhelming.

Now imagine that you are the master of your brain. Clearly articulate to your brain what you want to do in life, what dreams you have and acknowledge that your abilities are limitless. Once you start blocking the noises and fuel your brain with dominant positive thoughts aligned with the right actions, your brain will begin to function according to you.

Due to the complexities of our mental processes, we must make a conscious effort to avoid these noises. This is why achieving success in life can be so difficult.

Success is not just about tapping into the universe's energies; it is about aligning your actions with its divine timing to steer your destiny.

Surprisingly, many people die without fulfilling their goals and dreams, meaning only a small per cent becomes successful in life. What do these people do differently? They know how to shoo the noises and win big in life.

Inspiring Quotes

The human brain is an incredible pattern-matching machine.

> \- Jeff Bezos

Our greatest human adventure is the evolution of consciousness. We are in this life to enlarge the soul, liberate the spirit and light up the brain.

> \- Tom Robbins

The brain is like a muscle. When it is in use, we feel very good. Understanding is joyous.

> \- Carl Sagan

5

Too Many Forms of Success

SUCCESS IS A STATE of mind that differs from person to person. What constitutes success for you may mean 'nothing' to someone else.

No one can define success for you. In fact, you undermine yourself when you start measuring someone else's success against your own life path. For example, you might think, 'Oh look, what a lavish life he lives; he is a perfect example of success.'

No! This perspective is wrong. By doing this, you are setting boundaries for yourself. You are programming your brain to accept a particular 'limit'. You are telling yourself – this is it; this is where I want to reach. However, you are forgetting that you and that person are different.

What we read on social media, in magazines or see in interviews often does not reflect the complete reality. Let me give you an example. Suppose your favourite actor is Tom Cruise or Shah Rukh Khan; you might dream of living a life like theirs. There is nothing wrong with getting inspired, but when you start to rely on the morsels of information you get from the media and believe it to be the entire truth, you may begin to shape your day and pursue your goals based on that distorted perception.

This is similar to believing the 'woke up like this' and '#nofilter' photos you see on Instagram. I once came across a quote while scrolling through social media: 'Everyone has the same 24 hours in a day; what you do with it matters.'

Indeed, we all have 24 hours in a day, but they are not the same. For someone who is wealthy or a billionaire, their 24 hours may be filled with meetings, networking events and high-stakes decision-making. They often have a team of assistants and advisors to help them manage their time and prioritise tasks.

Their day might include travelling on private jets, attending exclusive events and engaging in leisure activities like golfing or yachting. They have access to luxurious amenities and services that save them time, such as private chefs, personal trainers and concierge services. Their financial resources allow them to delegate tasks and outsource responsibilities, enabling them to focus on activities that align with their goals and interests.

In contrast, someone who is poor or middle class may find their 24 hours consumed by long work hours, multiple jobs and commuting to and from work. They often have limited flexibility in their schedules due to rigid work hours and obligations to fulfil basic needs, such as childcare, household chores and paying bills.

Their day might be marked by financial stress, uncertainty about the future and the constant struggle to make ends meet. They may not have access to resources that can save them time or alleviate burdens, such as affordable childcare, transportation options or quality healthcare. Their limited financial resources may constrain their ability to pursue leisure activities or invest in personal development opportunities.

It is time to stop believing that everyone has the same 24 hours in a day. While we all have 24 hours, our circumstances are not the same. A major part of one's success is defined by these differences.

For instance, a wealthy child may inherit their family's business and property, allowing them to continue living a luxurious life, while a less fortunate child may need to work tirelessly to put food on the table.

Moreover, success may have a different meaning for you than what your parents or relatives think. Therefore it becomes important for you to define what 'success' means to you.

Success is a personal concept. While you can include your parents, spouse, friends, colleagues or relatives in your journey, it is crucial that their perspective on success does not overshadow your own understanding of it.

For instance, one of my cousins strongly believes that buying a fancy SUV with his earnings means he is successful. But for me, a trip to Dubai with my earnings represents success. While it is not my ultimate goal, it is one of the items on my bucket list. I do not think I would find happiness in spending a large sum of money on a car or a house. It is the mindset that matters.

Society often dictates that success is defined by owning a car or a house, wearing an uber-luxury brand or having a lavish wedding. However, success is more like aiming for a bullseye on a dartboard, but everyone's dartboard is a little different.

Success is fundamentally about setting meaningful goals and then working your tail off to achieve them. It feels like the joy you get when you accomplish something you have been aiming for, irrespective of whether it is a big or small milestone.

Here is the cool part: success is not just about reaching the finish line; it is also about enjoying the journey along the way. It is about the lessons you learn, the challenges you overcome and the friendships you build.

As I said, success looks different for everyone. It is not about comparing yourself to others or trying to live up to unrealistic standards. Success is discovering what makes you happy and fulfilled and pursuing it with everything you have.

Whether it means landing your dream job, starting a successful business, writing a book, acting, gaining admission into that particular college, finding happiness in your relationships or making a positive impact in your community, remember – it is your journey, your dartboard and your bullseye to hit.

And here is the catch! It keeps changing over time. Success is an infinite ladder. Once you reach a certain goal and feel successful, your mind will quickly set another target and the climb continues.

Our perceptions of success are shaped by our beliefs, values and experiences. What one person considers success may differ from another's view based on their unique perspectives and priorities.

Success, therefore, is subjective and can vary widely from person to person.

The way we think about ourselves and our goals influences our actions and behaviours. A positive and optimistic mindset can empower us to overcome challenges, persevere in the face of adversity and seize opportunities for growth and achievement. Conversely, a negative or defeatist mindset can hinder our progress and limit our potential for success.

True success is often measured by internal factors such as fulfilment, happiness and personal growth rather than external markers like wealth or status. When we align our goals with our values and find meaning and purpose in our pursuits, we experience a deeper sense of satisfaction and fulfilment.

However, I do not dismiss the importance of financial success. It is important, too, as dreams do not pay the bills. You need to work hard and smart to put food on the table.

Success is not a linear path; setbacks and failures are inevitable along the way. Maintaining a resilient and adaptable mindset allows us to learn from these challenges, pivot when necessary and continue moving forward despite obstacles.

So the basic step is to define your own meaning of success. For this I want you to write answers to these questions:

- List the names of five people (anyone – your family member, an actor, an athlete, a writer, anyone) you consider successful. Next to each name, write one reason why you believe they are successful.
  (Example: Elon Musk, because he owns a private jet.)

  _____
  _____

- If you were a successful person, what would you currently be doing?

  _____
  _____

- Write down five things or words that define success for you.

  _____

  _____

Consider your answers again and reflect on the type of success you desire in life. Let me help you understand the different categories of success.

- **Career success:** This type of success involves achieving professional goals, advancing in one's career, gaining recognition and attaining financial stability or prosperity. It also involves pursuing creative passions and finding recognition and fulfilment through artistic endeavours such as writing, painting, music or the performing arts. Examples of this type of success include landing a dream job, starting your own business, releasing a podcast or creating a music album.
- **Personal development success:** Personal development success encompasses growth in areas such as self-awareness, emotional intelligence, resilience and self-improvement. It involves becoming the best version of oneself and achieving a sense of fulfilment and purpose in life. Examples of personal development success include learning a new skill, cultivating good habits and quitting bad habits.
- **Financial success:** Financial success involves achieving financial security, independence and wealth accumulation. It requires managing finances effectively, investing wisely and attaining financial goals such as homeownership, retirement savings or financial freedom. Examples of financial success include purchasing a house, buying a vehicle and acquiring gold and diamonds.
- **Relationship success:** Relationship success involves cultivating healthy and fulfilling relationships with family, friends, romantic partners and colleagues. It requires fostering strong interpersonal connections, effective communication, trust, mutual respect and emotional intimacy. Examples of relationship success

include a homemaker striving for a harmonious relationship with a spouse, maintaining peace within the family and working towards a successful marriage with a partner.
- **Health and wellness success:** Health and wellness success focuses on achieving physical, mental and emotional well-being. It involves maintaining a healthy lifestyle, practising self-care, managing stress effectively and prioritising physical and mental health. Examples include healing yourself, losing or gaining weight and focusing on mental health.
- **Community and social impact success:** Community and social impact success means making a positive difference in the lives of others and contributing to the well-being of communities and society. Examples include volunteer work, philanthropy, advocacy and social activism.
- **Spiritual and inner success:** Spiritual and inner success involves achieving inner peace, fulfilment and spiritual growth. It includes exploring one's beliefs, values and purpose, practising mindfulness and cultivating a sense of connection with oneself, others and the universe.

You see, success can be pursued in diverse ways, reflecting the uniqueness of each individual's journey.

What truly matters when it comes to success is what matters to you. It is not about your family, spouse, relatives or friends; it is solely about you.

As I said, the definition of success changes over time and means different things to different people. It is not fixed and varies based on culture, society and personal experiences.

Success is about achieving goals and dreams, but what these goals are can vary depending on where you are and the time period you live in. For example, in ancient times, success might have meant conquering new lands or gaining wealth and power. In recent times, it might be seen as gaining knowledge, creating art, buying an asset, reaching a certain number of subscribers on

YouTube, making a positive impact on society or simply putting good food on the table every day.

Different places, cultures and societies have different perspectives on what constitutes success. In some cultures, success may be defined as having a large family or owning substantial property, while in others, it might mean pursuing education and following one's passions.

As societies evolve, so do our perceptions of success. During the Renaissance, for instance, success was often associated with creativity, learning and exploring new ideas. Today, success might be about finding balance in life, pursuing happiness or making a difference in the world.

When the COVID-19 pandemic shook the world in 2020, our only goal was to survive and stay alive. Some of us succeeded; some of us failed. You see, the idea of success completely changed at that time.

Ultimately, success is a state of mind, a flexible concept that evolves and means different things to different people, shaped by their culture, society and personal journey.

6

Identify Your Noise

NOISES DISRUPT OUR FOCUS and blur our vision. They are similar to having bugs buzzing around your head while you are trying to read a book in a park. There are two types of noises: internal noises and external noises.

Internal Noises

Internal noises refer to the thoughts, emotions and mental chatter that occur within our brain, affecting our focus, concentration and personal growth. These internal noises are subjective and can vary from person to person. Some of the most common internal noises are as follows:

- Self-doubt
- Fears
- Overthinking
- Insecurity
- Negative self-talk
- Traumas
- Limiting beliefs

Inner voices of uncertainty or a lack of confidence in one's abilities or decisions can lead to self-doubt. This self-doubt can undermine self-esteem and create obstacles to taking action or pursuing goals.

Feelings of apprehension, anxiety or worry about potential outcomes or future events can also arise. Such feelings can manifest as fear of failure, fear of rejection or fear of the unknown, and it can paralyse us from taking risks or stepping out of our comfort zones.

Critical or pessimistic inner dialogue can cause us to focus on our flaws, shortcomings or past mistakes. This negative self-talk can erode our self-esteem, increase stress levels and contribute to feelings of worthlessness or inadequacy.

Excessive rumination involves overanalysing past events, future scenarios or hypothetical situations. Overthinking can lead to mental fatigue, indecision and a lack of clarity, making it difficult to concentrate on the present moment or take decisive action.

Feelings of insecurity or inadequacy may arise concerning oneself, one's abilities or one's appearance. Insecurity can stem from comparisons with others, societal standards or past experiences of rejection or criticism.

The lingering effects of past traumas, negative experiences or unresolved emotional wounds can significantly impact our thoughts, emotions and behaviours. These influences may lead to patterns such as avoidance, hypervigilance or emotional reactivity.

Additionally, deep-seated beliefs or assumptions about ourselves, others or the world can constrain our perceptions and behaviours. Such limiting beliefs create self-imposed barriers to growth, success and fulfilment, preventing us from reaching our full potential.

External Noises

Internal noises are often fuelled by external noises. External noises encompass a wide range of external factors, influences and distractions that can impact our thoughts, emotions and actions. This type of noise is common among all of us. In fact, 98 per cent of people around the world who struggle to achieve success or reach their goals do so because of these external noises. External noises include the following:

- Inferiority complex
- People's opinions
- Financial concerns
- Responsibilities
- The internet

External noises often manifest as the tendency to compare ourselves to others. This comparison can involve achievements, possessions or appearances, frequently leading to feelings of inadequacy, jealousy or insecurity. Such constant comparison contributes to developing an inferiority complex, where individuals feel chronically inadequate or unworthy compared to others. These feelings can stem from societal standards, cultural expectations or past experiences of rejection and criticism.

Additionally, the opinions, judgements and expectations of others represent a common form of noise. Concerns about how we are perceived by friends, family members, colleagues or society at large can create pressure to conform or meet external standards of success and happiness.

Financial worries and pressures can lead to stress and anxiety. Concerns about money, debt, job security or meeting financial obligations can distract us from other important aspects of life and negatively impact our overall well-being, creating a significant barrier to our growth.

External noises often include the demands and responsibilities of daily life, such as work, family obligations, household chores or caregiving responsibilities.

The internet is a major source of distraction in today's digital age. It requires considerable determination to disconnect from the internet and focus on your tasks. Endless scrolling, notifications and information overload can fragment attention, foster comparison and contribute to feelings of inadequacy or

FOMO (fear of missing out). In fact, excessive exposure to online content can lead to an inferiority complex, which may ultimately result in depression.

Self-Doubt

Self-doubt occurs when we do not feel sure about ourselves. It is like having a little voice inside us that says, 'You cannot do it' or 'You are not good enough'. This feeling of uncertainty can stop us from reaching our goals and achieving success.

First, self-doubt makes us feel less confident. When we doubt ourselves, we do not believe we can do something well. Without confidence, it is hard to take risks or try new things. We might be afraid to speak up in class or try out for a sports team because we doubt our abilities.

Second, self-doubt makes us afraid of failing. We worry that if we attempt something and fail, it will prove that we are not good enough. So instead of taking chances, we play it safe and avoid situations where we might not succeed. However, this approach also means we miss valuable opportunities to learn and grow.

Third, self-doubt leads us to focus on our flaws instead of our strengths. We may compare ourselves to others and think we are not as smart, talented or capable as they are. This negative thinking can keep us from reaching our full potential and using our unique talents and abilities.

Moreover, self-doubt can make us indecisive. When we doubt ourselves, we second-guess our choices and hesitate to make decisions. We are afraid of making the wrong choice and facing criticism or disappointment. But this indecision can lead to missed opportunities and regrets.

Additionally, self-doubt can create a cycle of negativity. The more we doubt ourselves, the worse we feel about ourselves. It is like being trapped in a downward spiral that is difficult to escape.

So how can we overcome self-doubt and achieve success?

First, we need to recognise that everyone experiences self-doubt from time to time. It is a normal feeling but does not have to control us. We can challenge negative thoughts and replace them with positive affirmations.

Second, we should focus on our strengths and celebrate our accomplishments, no matter how small they may seem. By building self-confidence and believing in ourselves, we can overcome self-doubt and face new challenges with courage and determination.

Third, we can surround ourselves with supportive friends and family who believe in us, which can make a significant difference. Encouragement from a strong support system can help us overcome self-doubt and stay motivated, even when things get tough.

Self-doubt can be a barrier to success, but it does not have to hold us back. By recognising our worth, focusing on our strengths and seeking support from others, we can overcome self-doubt and achieve our goals. Remember, we are capable of more than we think, and we can accomplish great things with perseverance and self-belief.

Everyone knows J.K. Rowling, the author who transformed how people read books with her creation of the Harry Potter series. She wrote her first book *Rabbit* at the age of six, which was a story about a rabbit. By the age of eleven, she had completed her first novel about seven cursed diamonds and the people who owned them. Isn't that interesting?

Before the magic of Harry Potter captured the hearts of millions, Rowling faced a series of setbacks that would have discouraged even the most resilient souls. Twelve publishers rejected the manuscript of *Harry Potter and the Philosopher's Stone*. Twelve! But Rowling refused to give in to despair.

You can sense the weight of Rowling's self-doubt, the nagging voice in her head questioning her worth as a writer. It is hard to imagine now, isn't it?

The woman who brought Hogwarts to life doubted her abilities. But Rowling is human, just like you and me. Her battle with self-doubt made her journey all the more inspiring. Instead of succumbing to despair, she transformed her doubts into fuel for her determination.

With each rejection, Rowling's resolve grew stronger. She said in an interview, 'It is impossible to live without failing at something unless you live so cautiously that you might as well not have lived at all.'

But Rowling did not just overcome her self-doubt; she transformed it into a source of strength. She poured her heart and soul into her writing, refusing to let rejection define her. In 1997, her perseverance paid off when Bloomsbury decided to publish the Harry Potter series.

From humble beginnings, Rowling became one of the bestselling authors of all time, beloved by people of all ages, cultures and countries. She proved that you should not allow self-doubt to deter you from pursuing your dreams. You need to believe in yourself and shoo the noises to succeed in life.

Fears are like ghosts. If you are scared of ghosts, then ghosts will haunt you.

Imagine how scared you feel when you go to the washroom at night in complete darkness. You might believe someone is walking behind you, so you start walking faster. But the moment you take a deep breath and look around, you realise there is nothing there – it was all in your head. This is exactly how you can confront your fears.

I do not deny the presence of supernatural energies around us, but these energies do not bother us unless we disturb them.

When we hear ghost stories or watch horror movies, our minds often start to play tricks on us. We become scared and begin imagining things that may not even exist.

It all comes down to our brains.

Ghosts thrive on those who hesitate – those with weak minds, time-wasters, self-doubters and overthinkers. To eliminate fear from your mind, you must rid yourself of these habits.

Fear is a powerful noise that keeps us from reaching our full potential and achieving success. It acts as a barrier, clouding our vision and preventing us from seizing opportunities. However, facing our fears head-on is essential for personal growth and unlocking new possibilities in life.

There are many types of fears that can hinder our progress.

One common fear is the fear of failure. We often worry about making mistakes or not meeting expectations, which leads us to avoid taking risks and stepping outside our comfort zones. This fear can paralyse us, preventing us from pursuing our dreams and exploring new paths. Imagine, if you do not try, how will you know what the future holds for you? And if you do fail, you can always try again!

Thomas Edison, the famous inventor and scientist credited with creating the light bulb and the motion picture camera, was once asked about his many failures and why he did not give up. He responded, 'I have not failed. I have just found 10,000 ways that will not work.' Each failure brings us closer to success if we continue to try. We simply need to start seeing things from a positive perspective. I will discuss this further later in the book.

One common type of fear is the fear of rejection. We often worry about being judged or criticised by others, which leads us to hold back from expressing ourselves authentically or sharing our ideas and talents with the world. This fear of rejection can limit our opportunities for growth and connection, trapping us in a cycle of self-doubt and isolation. For example, if J.K. Rowling had let her fear of rejection stop her, she would never have sent her manuscript to a publisher or might have given up after just one or two rejections.

Another significant fear is the fear of the unknown. Many of us feel anxious about the future and are apprehensive about entering unfamiliar territory. This fear can keep us stuck in our comfort zones, clinging to what is familiar and avoiding change – even if it means missing out on exciting opportunities for personal and professional development.

Despite the challenges that fear presents, it is important to confront and overcome it. As Nelson Mandela famously said, 'I learned that courage was not the absence of fear, but the triumph over it.'

By facing our fears, we discover our inner strength and resilience, which empower us to pursue our goals with confidence and determination. Furthermore, confronting fear allows us to expand our horizons and unlock new opportunities for growth and success. When we step outside our comfort zones and face our fears, we uncover hidden talents, passions and possibilities that we never knew existed.

Overthinking

Sometimes, our brains just cannot seem to turn off, right?

It feels like we are stuck in this loop of thoughts, analysing every little thing to death. And you know what? This overthinking is holding us back from reaching our full potential. Think about it.

We spend so much time worrying about what might go wrong or how people might perceive us that we forget to actually live our lives. It is as if we are trapped in this mental quicksand, sinking deeper and deeper into our thoughts.

But here's the thing: we need to stop overthinking. Seriously, it is time to break free from that cycle of doubt and indecision. Because guess what? Life is passing us by while we are busy second-guessing ourselves.

I mean, think about all the amazing things we could accomplish if we just trusted ourselves a little more and stopped overthinking every little detail. We would be unstoppable!

You know, I love a quote by Mark Twain: 'I have had a lot of worries in my life, most of which never happened.' Is that not the truth? We waste so much energy worrying about things that never even come to pass.

And then there is Eleanor Roosevelt, who famously stated, 'Do one thing every day that scares you.' Now, I am not suggesting we have to go skydiving (unless that is your thing), but we should strive to push ourselves beyond our comfort zones.

Insecurity

Let us explore the topic of insecurity, that nagging feeling that often gnaws at us, making us doubt ourselves and our abilities. It acts like an invisible barrier, preventing us from reaching our full potential, growing and achieving success.

But here is the thing: it is time to break free from the grip of insecurity and step into our greatness.

First, let us understand how insecurity acts as a barrier in our lives. When we feel insecure, we continuously doubt ourselves and our values. This self-doubt can lead us to hesitate in pursuing opportunities or taking risks, as we believe we are not good enough. We often compare ourselves to others, which can worsen our insecurities.

For example, consider a talented artist who is new to the field. This artist may feel too insecure to showcase their work, fearing that others will ridicule their art or compare it unfavourably to that of established artists. Their insecurity not only holds them back from sharing their talents with the world but also limits their growth as an artist.

We cannot compare ourselves with others. Each person has different abilities and capabilities. Everyone follows a unique path and journey. Just because you share something in common with someone else – such as a profession, talent, background, caste, religion, gender, society or area of interest – does not mean you and that person have the same abilities, perspectives and thought processes.

Although a rose and a lotus are both flowers, you cannot compare them simply because they belong to the same category. They are inherently different.

In addition to our professional lives, insecurity can also affect our relationships with others. When we feel insecure, we may struggle to trust or open up to others, fearing judgement or abandonment. This can lead to feelings of loneliness and isolation, preventing us from forming meaningful connections with those around us.

Most breakups occur due to insecurities, as these insecurities can lead to trust issues. When you feel you are not good enough for your partner, you may worry they will leave you for someone else simply because you believe another person is somehow better than you.

It is crucial to stop being insecure. This noise can damage everything, creating barriers to personal and professional growth and success. Insecurity often robs us of our happiness and peace of mind. It traps us in a cycle of self-doubt and negativity, preventing us from fully enjoying life and pursuing our passions.

For instance, someone constantly insecure about their appearance may avoid social situations or feel anxious in public settings, leading to missed opportunities for joy and fulfilment.

Moreover, insecurity holds us back from reaching our full potential. When we doubt ourselves, we may settle for less than we deserve or avoid taking risks that could lead to growth and success.

So how do we stop being insecure and break free from these barriers?

It begins with recognising our self-worth and embracing self-acceptance. We need to challenge the negative thoughts and beliefs that fuel our insecurity and replace them with affirmations of self-love and confidence.

It is important to surround ourselves with supportive and uplifting people who believe in us and encourage us to pursue our goals rather than those who might ruin our aspirations, spoil our progress or bring us down. The company we keep matters a lot. It can make or break our insecurity. By building a strong support network, we can gain the courage to step out of our comfort zones and pursue our dreams with determination and resilience.

Negative Self-Talk

You know that little voice inside our heads that sometimes tells us we are not good enough or that we cannot do something. Negative self-talk can be a major barrier to our growth, success and happiness.

Negative self-talk is basically the way we communicate with ourselves internally. Those thoughts and beliefs that make us feel we are not smart, talented or worthy. While it may sound similar to feelings of insecurity, it is even worse.

For example, imagine you have a big presentation coming up at work. Instead of telling yourself, 'I have prepared for this, and I can do it', your mind might chime in with negative messages such as 'I am going to mess up' or 'Nobody will take me seriously'. That is a clear example of negative self-talk in action.

When we constantly tell ourselves that we are not good enough or cannot accomplish something, we begin to believe it. It is like planting seeds of doubt in our minds, which can grow into large, thorny bushes that block our path to success.

Negative self-talk also undermines our confidence and self-esteem. When we constantly criticise ourselves and focus on our flaws, it erodes our self-confidence and makes us doubt our worth. It is similar to wearing a pair of glasses that only allow us to see our shortcomings and failures while obscuring our strengths and successes.

Eleanor Roosevelt once said, 'No one can make you feel inferior without your consent.' It is up to us to take control of our thoughts and not allow negative self-talk to dictate our lives. Instead, we should replace those negative thoughts with positive affirmations and beliefs that uplift us and empower us to pursue our dreams. In a previous chapter, I mentioned that we need to treat our brains like our servants. Stopping negative self-talk is essential because it directly affects our mental and emotional well-being.

When we constantly bombard ourselves with negative thoughts, it takes a toll on our mental health, leaving us feeling stressed, anxious and unhappy.

By cultivating a positive mindset and challenging negative self-talk, we can improve our overall well-being and lead happier, more fulfilling lives.

Traumas

Traumas can be compared to heavy backpacks that we carry with us, filled with painful experiences that weigh us down and make it hard to move forward. Sometimes, we may not even be aware of this backpack and the burdens it holds. Traumas come in all shapes and sizes, and each one leaves its mark on us in different ways.

One of the most common forms of trauma is childhood trauma. It acts like a shadow that follows us from our earliest days, caused by things like abuse, neglect or growing up in a chaotic home. Childhood trauma shapes how we see ourselves and the world around us, frequently making it difficult to trust others or feel safe. Surprisingly, studies show that as many as 15 per cent of girls and 6 per cent of boys develop post-traumatic stress disorder (PTSD) as a result of childhood trauma.

Grief and loss trauma can be incredibly challenging. Losing someone we love – whether it is a family member, a friend or even a pet – can feel like a punch to the gut. It leaves us feeling empty and lost, struggling to make sense of our emotions and find a way forward. I have experienced this myself, and I can only say it is a dangerous place to be. I am grateful that I found my way out of it.

Another difficult type of trauma is related to accidents and injuries. Imagine being involved in a car crash or surviving a natural disaster. These experiences can shake us to our core, leaving us with scars, both seen and unseen, that take time to heal.

And let us also consider medical trauma. Experiencing surgeries or facing serious illnesses can be frightening and overwhelming. It often feels like we have lost control, with our bodies betraying us during our most vulnerable moments.

Then there is military and combat trauma. For those who have served in the military or participated in combat, the sights and experiences they have encountered can continue to haunt them long after returning home. It feels like they are carrying the weight of the world on their shoulders, with memories that never seem to fade.

Interpersonal trauma is a challenging topic to discuss. It encompasses experiences such as violence, assault or betrayal by others. Whether physical or emotional, the pain runs deep and can leave lasting scars that may never fully heal.

And lastly, systemic trauma. This one is a bit different because it addresses not just individual experiences but also the collective pain of entire communities or populations. Think about things like genocide, slavery or institutional discrimination. These events leave wounds that span generations, shaping the lives of everyone they touch.

But here is the thing: no matter what kind of trauma we have been through, it is important to remember that healing is possible. It is like setting down a heavy backpack and taking a deep breath. While the healing process may not happen overnight and can require significant effort, it is definitely worthwhile. Trauma, if not handled and healed properly, can either make you sensitive or leave you numb.

As Maya Angelou, the famous author and civil rights activist, once said, 'You may encounter many defeats, but you must not be defeated.'

We are stronger than we realise. With the right support and resources, we can overcome even the most challenging obstacles.

Limited Beliefs

The phrase 'The sky is the limit' is familiar to many of us; it serves as a reminder that our potential is as vast and boundless as the sky above. But what happens when we let limiting beliefs cloud our view of that limitless horizon?

Let us discuss these limiting beliefs – those pesky doubts and fears that prevent us from reaching for the stars. They are like clouds that obscure the brilliance of the sky, casting shadows on our dreams and aspirations.

Limited beliefs act like invisible walls we build around ourselves, often without realising it. Perhaps you have heard that inner voice telling you things like, 'This is impossible to achieve', 'I cannot do it', 'This is beyond my potential' or 'I could never be as successful as they are'.

But let me tell you something: those limiting beliefs are nothing more than lies we tell ourselves. They are false accusations we make about our capabilities.

These beliefs often stem from past experiences, societal conditioning or negative self-talk. They can hold us back from achieving our full potential, pursuing our goals or experiencing personal growth and fulfilment.

Some common examples of limiting beliefs include the following:

- I do not have enough time.
- I am not good enough.
- I do not deserve success.
- I am too old or too young to pursue my dreams.
- I am not smart or talented enough.
- I am destined to fail.
- Money is hard to come by.
- I am not lovable.
- The kind of success he/she has is impossible for me to get.
- The kind of relationship they have is not meant for me.
- This is impossible for me.

These beliefs play a significant role in shaping our behaviours, decisions and attitudes, often creating self-imposed barriers to our progress and happiness. Over time, these beliefs become deeply embedded in our subconscious, influencing how we perceive ourselves and the world around us.

Therefore, addressing these limiting beliefs with a practical mindset is important.

Awareness

The first step in overcoming limiting beliefs is to become aware of them. Pay attention to your thoughts, especially in situations where you feel stuck or doubt your abilities. Journaling can be a helpful tool for identifying recurring negative thought patterns.

Challenge

Once you have identified a limiting belief, challenge its validity. Ask yourself the following questions:
- What evidence supports this belief?
- What evidence contradicts it?
- How does this belief serve or hinder me?
- What would happen if I let go of this belief?

By critically examining your beliefs, you can start to loosen their grip on your mindset.

Reframe

Reframing involves replacing limiting beliefs with more empowering perspectives. Instead of saying 'I am not good enough', you might reframe it as 'I am capable of learning and improving'. Look for evidence of your strengths, achievements and past successes to support these new beliefs. Choose affirmations that directly counteract your limiting beliefs. For example, if you struggle with self-doubt, affirmations like 'I believe in myself and my abilities' can help reinforce your confidence and self-assurance. I will discuss this process in one of the chapters later in the book and explain how I work on it to overcome limiting beliefs.

Behavioural Changes

Actively engaging in behaviours that align with your new beliefs can strengthen them over time. Challenge yourself to step outside your comfort zone, seize new opportunities and embrace failure as a learning experience rather than as validation of your limiting beliefs.

Practise Self-Compassion

Be patient and kind to yourself throughout this process. Overcoming limiting beliefs takes time and effort, and setbacks are a natural part of growth. Treat yourself with the same compassion and understanding that you would offer a friend facing similar challenges.

By consistently challenging and reframing your limiting beliefs, you can cultivate a more empowering mindset that enables you to pursue your aspirations with confidence and resilience. Remember, personal growth is an ongoing journey, and every step you take towards overcoming limiting beliefs brings you closer to realising your full potential.

Inferiority Complex

Imagine you are in class, struggling to understand a math problem while your friend solves it effortlessly. You start to feel like you will never grasp the concept. Now consider another scenario: you attend a family function where all your relatives arrive in their fancy cars, but you show up in a rickshaw. You feel embarrassed, even though no one has said anything negative to you. That is your inferiority complex talking!

We all have our strengths and weaknesses.

This inferiority complex can develop early and is often rooted in childhood experiences.

Can you recall moments from your childhood when a relative or cousin showed off their fancy, expensive dress or footwear, making you feel embarrassed for not having the same? Or when you arrived at a family function in a rickshaw or tuk-tuk and tried to hide it because others had their own vehicles? Or when a group of friends pulled out an expensive perfume, while you were left with an ₹80 perfume, making you feel too humiliated to use it in front of them? This is the complex I am talking about.

Feelings of worthlessness, incompetence, inadequacy and embarrassment form the foundation of an inferiority complex.

Michael Jordan, one of the greatest basketball players of all time, once said, 'I have missed more than 9,000 shots in my career. I have lost almost 300 games. Twenty-six times, I have been trusted to take the game-winning shot and missed. I have failed over and over and over again in my life. And that is why I succeed, because I believed in myself.'

This serves as a powerful reminder that even the best face setbacks. What truly matters is how we bounce back.

Now, think about your favourite superhero. They all have flaws, right? Spider-Man makes mistakes, Batman experiences doubts and Wonder Woman faces challenges. But guess what? They still save the day! What is the moral here? You need to focus on your strengths and keep going, no matter what.

Now, let us talk about our superpowers. Maybe you are great at making people laugh, creating amazing drawings or helping your friends when they feel down. These are the unique talents that make you special!

Sure, we might not be perfect, but who is? Even the Mona Lisa has imperfections if you look closely! The key is to embrace what makes us different and use it to shine bright like a diamond.

Remember, you are amazing just the way you are. Surround yourself with people who lift you up, keep believing in yourself and never stop reaching for the stars!

In the words of Dr Seuss, 'Today you are you, that is truer than true. There is no one alive who is youer than you.'

People's Opinions

'No, you cannot do it' – this is the loudest noise you hear in life. It is the cause of all the internal noises you harbour within you.

It is like being at a party and hesitating to dance because you are worried about what others might think. We hold ourselves back, fearing judgement or ridicule. But you know what?

Imagine you have a big dream, such as becoming a writer, an artist or starting your own business. But then, everyone around you says, 'Oh, that is too risky' or 'You will never make it'. It is as if they are building a wall of doubt around you. But you know, some of the most successful people in history faced similar doubts and criticisms.

For instance, Amitabh Bachchan, the legendary actor of Indian cinema, also encountered rejection on his path to success.

When he first entered the film industry in the 1970s, filmmakers and producers believed his voice was too deep and unconventional for leading roles. They thought his voice would not resonate well with audiences and might hinder his potential as an actor.

He auditioned for a voice-over job at All India Radio (AIR), India's national radio broadcaster. During the audition, the selectors deemed his voice unsuitable for radio broadcasting and rejected him.

This rejection could have been disheartening for Amitabh Bachchan, but he did not let it deter him. Instead, he persevered and continued to pursue his passion for acting. Despite facing initial setbacks, Amitabh Bachchan's determination, talent and hard work eventually propelled him to superstardom in the Indian film industry.

Amitabh Bachchan's iconic deep voice became one of his trademarks and significantly contributed to his on-screen persona. People still mimic his famous dialogues, such as '*Rishte me toh hum tumhare baap hote hai, naam hai Shahenshah*', '*Don ko pakadna mushkil hi nahi, namumkin hai*' and '*Hum jahan khade hote hai, line wahi se shuru hoti hai*'. I bet you can hear his voice while reading these lines.

That is how you turn a setback into your greatest victory.

He defied the odds and proved his critics wrong, becoming one of the most celebrated actors in the history of Indian cinema.

This incident serves as a powerful reminder that rejection and criticism are often part of the journey to success. Amitabh Bachchan's story inspires us to stay resilient, believe in ourselves and embrace our unique qualities, even when others doubt us.

When we let other people's opinions dictate our actions and decisions, we are not living authentically. Instead, we are living according to someone else's script rather than writing our own.

Remember, your story is *your* story, and only you should have the power to write it.

The only opinion that truly matters is the one you have of yourself. Trust yourself, believe in your dreams and do not let anyone dim your light.

Financial Concerns and Responsibilities

Life can sometimes throw us curveballs, like bills to pay, loans to manage and everyday expenses that keep adding up. It is like we are juggling numerous financial responsibilities while trying to chase our dreams, and sometimes, it feels as if we are stuck in a never-ending cycle.

Suppose you have an amazing idea for starting your own business or pursuing a passion project, but then you start to worry about money. Can you afford to take that risk? What if you fail? These concerns can hold us back from taking that leap of faith.

Every successful person you admire has faced financial struggles at some point. Take Walt Disney, for example. Did you know he was once fired from a newspaper because they said he lacked imagination? When he first started Disneyland, he also encountered financial difficulties. But did he give up? No! He continued to believe in his dreams and worked hard to make them a reality.

So what can we do when financial concerns start creeping in and holding us back?

Well, first, it is important to have a plan. Take a good look at your finances to determine what you need to do to make ends meet while still pursuing your dreams. This might involve cutting back on certain expenses or exploring creative ways to save money.

Second, do not hesitate to seek help. Whether it is reaching out to your parents, consulting a financial advisor, finding a mentor who has navigated similar challenges or even just talking to friends and family about your goals, having a strong support system can make all the difference.

And finally, remember that success does not happen overnight. It takes time, patience, perseverance and sometimes failure.

Life is filled with risks. You cannot just sit on the shore, worrying about what might happen if your ship sinks. You need to dive into the ocean and confront those challenges head-on.

I understand that financial concerns and responsibilities are practical noises and can keep people stuck for a long time. 'I cannot relocate because my family needs me', 'I cannot attend my dream college because I cannot afford it and do not want to burden my parents', 'I am not getting an investor for my startup', 'My family forced me to get married, so I cannot pursue my dreams now'. The issues are endless, but there is one solution: find a way because where there is a will, there is a way!

Yes, I strongly believe every problem has a solution or an alternative. I have often heard people say things like, 'God is unfair to me', 'The universe is unfair to me', 'I am not lucky' or 'I am not destined for success'.

But the truth is that these notions are misguided.

God or the universe is never unfair; it simply expects you to seek the right path that will be better for you in the long run. Obstacles and hurdles are merely tests to help you discover your own strength and potential. Whenever you encounter any noise that brings you down and demotivates you, remember that the universe is testing your resilience and determination.

It is like saying, 'Hey, let us see what you are made of!'

Have you ever faced a problem or challenge that initially seemed impossible to overcome? However, as you confronted it directly, you realised you were stronger and more capable than you thought. That is the point I am trying to make!

Every obstacle we face presents an opportunity to grow, learn, and become better versions of ourselves. It is similar to enduring a tough workout at the gym – while it may be difficult, you feel stronger and more confident afterwards, right?

So instead of getting discouraged when things do not go as planned, let us view these moments as opportunities to prove ourselves. We should embrace the challenges, learn from them and emerge even stronger on the other side!

The Internet

The internet is the ultimate big daddy of all noises.

We live in a digital age where our day begins and ends with the internet.

How often have you found yourself scrolling through social media for hours instead of doing something productive or spending time with friends? Yeah, we have all been there!

The thing is, the internet is filled with endless content vying for our attention – memes, videos, news, you name it. While some of this content can be fun and entertaining, it can also distract us from things that matter, like pursuing our goals or spending quality time with loved ones.

Have you ever noticed how easy it is to compare ourselves to others online? We are often exposed to highlight reels on social media, making it easy to feel like we are not measuring up. But the truth is, most of what we see online is just a snapshot of someone else's life, not the complete picture.

And let us not forget the issue of information overload! There is an overwhelming amount of content on the internet, which can be difficult to process. It is like trying to drink from a fire hose – you simply cannot take it all in!

For instance, let us talk about fancy travel videos. The images of luxury five-star hotels, business-class flight seats and expensive car rides often lead people to believe that this is the only right way to enjoy a holiday. As a result, many delay their travel plans simply because they cannot afford a water villa or a business-class ticket. In fact, I have noticed that some people avoid sharing updates about their travels on social media because they feel embarrassed to admit they are travelling by sleeper-class train or on a non-air-conditioned bus.

It is wrong.

I am a travel blogger and have been hosted by some top hospitality brands, including Hotel Pullman, Novotel, Hyatt Regency, Taj and more. Many so-called 'influencers' are also hosted, meaning they do not pay for their stay and meals. As you plan your vacation, it is important to remember that you are spending your hard-earned money. Do not let a stranger's Instagram feed dictate your #VacationGoals.

If you can afford a train or bus ticket and your bank balance allows for decent accommodation, take that trip. Do not let the noise from social media fill your ears with unrealistic expectations. Instead, define your own set of voices that you want to listen to and do not let these strange noises bother you.

There is a fine line between 'getting inspired' and 'developing a complex' or 'feeling envious'.

It is perfectly okay to feel inspired and push your limits, but delaying or cancelling things just because someone else is doing it differently is unwise.

What you see on social media is often not true.

In the first week of January 2024, Gulmarg did not receive any snowfall. The landscape resembled barren land devoid of snow or greenery. But on Instagram, content creators were putting out reels with captions like 'Kashmir right now' and 'Gulmarg right now'. It was highly misleading to the audience. One of my cousins even planned a trip to Gulmarg to experience the winter wonderland but returned feeling extremely disappointed.

It is disappointing to see how social media can create such noise, often disrupting personal relationships as well.

Last month, one of my life coaching mentees shared with me that his girlfriend broke up with him because her friend's boyfriend planned a fancy proposal for her. In contrast, my mentee simply asked her to marry him while they were sitting in a car. Now, they are no longer getting married because the girl believes she will not be able to adjust to him and be 'happy'. She feels this way because he is not very expressive and does not plan things like the elaborate proposals she sees on Instagram, which frustrates her.

Can you imagine how silly this reason is? How can people assume that the perfectly happy couples we see on the internet have no problems? Everything we see online is often curated and may not reflect reality, even down to the tears!

It is funny because I cannot cry in front of a camera. Imagine being heartbroken, feeling like your life is falling apart and wanting to cry. So you open the camera, press the record button and then start crying.

Silly, isn't it? Well, it is actually clickbait – a type of content designed to attract attention and get users to click on it.

This tendency to perform emotionally is not just relevant in personal relationships; it can also create barriers to professional growth and academic success.

Social media is like a double-edged sword. On one hand, it keeps us connected and entertained; on the other, it can affect our mental health and bring us down.

We are constantly bombarded with information we do not even need. My schedule is hectic as I am a writer, professional life coach and consultant, tarot guide and travel content creator, so I rarely step into my kitchen to cook; yet I find myself watching fancy cooking reels. What happens in that moment? I have just wasted 60 seconds of my time on something unproductive while the creator of that video gains another view at the expense of my time.

There is constant pressure to be online, check notifications and keep up with the latest trends. You will be surprised to know that about 694,000 hours of video are streamed by YouTube users every single minute. Imagine!

We often assume that the internet is free, but the truth is that it costs us one of the most valuable things in our lives – our focus.

We do not realise that mindless scrolling on the web can seriously impact our concentration and mental health. It is like a never-ending loop of comparison, FOMO and negativity, leaving us feeling drained and unhappy.

That is where the trouble starts. We start to feel like we are not good enough or that we are missing out on all the fun everyone else seems to be having. This creates constant pressure to conform to an idealised version of ourselves that is simply not real.

Before we realise it, we are spending too much time online, feeling lonelier and more disconnected than ever. It is as if we are trapped in a cycle of seeking validation and approval from others, even though we know deep down that it is not healthy.

The internet is a good servant but a bad master.

My Father, My Hero

What hurts the most? When your parents, the ones you trust deeply, start to doubt your abilities.

This incident occurred in the early 1980s, long before the internet or mobile phones became a thing. My dad was a topper in both school and college, yet his father doubted whether he would secure a good government job.

My dad dreamt of becoming a forest ranger. He earned a master's degree in botany with the intention of pursuing that dream. However, as he neared the completion of his degree, my grandfather began pressuring him to find a job.

While preparing for the UPSC exam, the entrance exam required to become a forest ranger, he was also studying for the banking exam. He did not share this with anyone because people believed it was impossible to qualify. As the eldest son in the family, he felt he had responsibilities that prevented him from leaving the city.

Meanwhile, my grandfather's cousin visited our home and mentioned that he had found a perfect job for my dad – as a worker in a nearby cotton factory.

Initially, my dad refused to take the job, but my grandfather insisted that he accept it out of respect for family expectations. As a result, my dad joined the factory and missed his opportunity to take the UPSC exam.

He worked there for just one day before quitting.

My grandfather was furious. He wanted my dad to start earning rather than 'sitting at home and listening to the radio'.

The uncle who got him the job came to our house, upset and said to my grandfather, 'I think he has gone crazy because he topped his MSc. The job I found for him is one he could never hope to get otherwise. It pays well according to industry standards. Maybe he dreams of getting a government job in a bank like my son, but that is unrealistic for him. Tell him to face reality and ask him to return to the factory.'

These words struck a chord with my dad. He felt insulted. My father was a genius; I am not just saying this because he was my dad. What followed next truly showcased his remarkable abilities.

He entered six government bank exams and qualified for all of them. One after another, the results came in and my dad proudly handed all the copies to my grandfather to show to that uncle.

Although my dad gave up on his dream of becoming a forest ranger, he achieved another dream. In the early 1980s, landing a government job, especially in banking, was considered a golden opportunity. Even later, when he recounted this incident to me, he said that he never regretted not becoming a forest ranger. In fact, he was grateful that if that uncle had not made so much noise, he might never have achieved this victory in his life.

I want to share this with you because we often seek inspiration from famous personalities, forgetting that inspiration is everywhere, even in our homes.

Many of us have toxic relatives who poke and prod us about our job packages, marriage and children. They do not genuinely care; they simply belittle us. My dad never disrespected that uncle, but his success in securing his desired job served as his answer to all the humiliation from that uncle.

He did not stop there; he transformed his life from having just a single bed to an entire mansion filled with amenities. It is truly a real-life rags-to-riches story. My dad succeeded because he believed in himself and did not allow the noises to block his way.

Questions to Answer

- Why do you feel you are not good enough?
  _____

- Who in your social circle do you think is better than you, and why?
  _____

- Are there any childhood traumas or limiting beliefs that you cannot overcome?
  _____

- If there were no obligations of society, family, finances or age, and no fear of judgement or failure, what is the one thing you would do towards your dream life or career?
  _____

- When was the last time you felt proud of yourself, and why?
  _____

Inspiring Quotes

Doubt kills more dreams than failure ever will.

- Suzy Kassem

Fear is only as deep as the mind allows.

- Japanese Proverb

Don't let the noise of others' opinions drown out your own inner voice.

- Steve jobs

Obstacles do not have to stop you. If you run into a wall, do not turn around and give up. Figure out how to climb it, go through it or work around it.

- Michael Jordan

Believe in yourself and all that you are. Know that there is something inside you that is greater than any obstacle.

- Christian D. Larson

7

Heal Emotional Wounds

EMOTIONAL WOUNDS ARE DEEP-SEATED hurts, the invisible pain we carry within ourselves. These stem from experiences such as rejection, betrayal, loss or trauma. Unlike physical wounds that are visible and tangible, emotional wounds exist within our psyche, impacting our thoughts, emotions and behaviours. These wounds can be triggered by a variety of life events and relationships, leaving lasting imprints on our mental well-being and hindering us from achieving our life's purpose and goals.

Imagine someone you really trusted betrays you. It hurts deep down, doesn't it? Or maybe you have experienced the loss of a loved one, leaving you with a sense that a piece of your heart is missing. Similarly, being humiliated or experiencing sexual violation can leave you unable to escape those painful memories.

These are the kinds of wounds we are discussing, among many others. It is impossible to compile an exhaustive list of emotional wounds, as each person's sensitivities are unique.

Do not think of your emotional wounds as weaknesses. Instead, let your scars be the constellations of strength, guiding and empowering you to rise. Your wounds are not your weakness; they are simply noises you need to tune out.

So how do we do that? By healing ourselves.

Just like physical wounds, emotional wounds can heal too. All it takes is time, patience and a bit of tender loving care – it is like giving yourself a big emotional hug!

Heal Emotional Wounds

Healing does not mean you have completely moved on from your emotional wounds; it means they no longer control you, bother you or block your path to growth, success and happiness.

Many people believe that therapy is the only solution for healing emotional wounds. While it can be beneficial, if you feel you need professional help, do not hesitate to seek it out.

But that is not the only solution. Keep it as a last resort. First, try to heal yourself.

But how do we do it?

The first step is to accept and acknowledge our feelings. It is okay to feel sad, angry or hurt. These feelings are valid, and it is important to express them rather than bottle them up inside. You must confront your feelings in order to heal from them, and for that, you need to identify the root cause.

Emotional wounds can take many forms, including:

- **Rejection**: Experiencing rejection, whether in relationships, friendships or professional settings, can leave profound emotional scars. Rejection triggers feelings of unworthiness, inadequacy and abandonment, affecting our self-esteem and confidence.
- **Betrayal**: Betrayal occurs when someone we trust violates that trust, causing deep emotional pain and disillusionment. Betrayal can take many forms, including infidelity, deceit or broken promises, and it shatters our sense of security and trust in others.
- **Loss**: Losing someone or something we hold dear, whether through death, separation or life transitions, can result in profound grief and sadness. The pain of loss manifests as a deep emotional wound, leaving us feeling empty, bereft and longing for what we once had.
- **Trauma**: Traumatic experiences, such as abuse, violence or accidents, can inflict lasting emotional wounds that impact our sense of safety, trust and well-being. Trauma disrupts our ability to regulate emotions and cope with stress, often leading to symptoms of anxiety, depression and PTSD.

These emotional wounds have far-reaching consequences that permeate every aspect of our lives. They influence our thoughts, beliefs, relationships and behaviours, shaping our perceptions of ourselves and the world around us. The impact of emotional wounds can manifest in various ways:

- **Low self-esteem**: Emotional wounds erode our sense of self-worth and value, leading to feelings of inadequacy, self-doubt and self-criticism. We may internalise negative beliefs about ourselves, viewing ourselves through the lens of our past experiences and perceived shortcomings.
- **Impaired relationships**: Emotional wounds affect our ability to form and maintain healthy relationships. We may struggle with trust issues, fear of intimacy and difficulty expressing emotions openly and authentically. Our past wounds may sabotage our relationships, leading to conflicts, misunderstandings and emotional distance.
- **Emotional dysregulation**: Emotional wounds disrupt our ability to regulate emotions effectively. We may experience intense mood swings, emotional outbursts or even numbness as a result of unresolved pain and trauma. Our emotional responses might become disproportionate to the situation, causing distress and instability in our daily lives.
- **Limiting beliefs and behaviours**: Emotional wounds can lead to limiting beliefs and behaviours that prevent us from reaching our full potential. As a result, we may engage in self-sabotaging patterns, avoid taking risks or resist opportunities for growth and change due to fear of failure or rejection.

Emotional wounds can be deeply ingrained and pervasive, but healing is possible through time, self-awareness and intentional effort.

Once you identify the root cause of your emotional wound, start with acceptance.

We often run away from our emotional wounds, believing that facing them makes us appear weak. We sometimes pretend to be numb and avoid our feelings because we do not want to cry anymore.

I understand this because I have been there and done that. Trust me when I say this: it does not help. It is like brushing dirt under a carpet. What happens then? Eventually, there will be no space left to brush the dirt under that carpet, and you must clear it all at once. While the dirt sits beneath the carpet, it may attract unwanted insects and cause the floor or carpet to rot.

Avoiding emotional wounds and refusing to accept them are essentially the same. Eventually, these repressed feelings explode all at once, like a firecracker, causing your world to fall apart. You cannot even imagine the extent of the damage they have caused while being stored inside you.

I did the same when I lost my parents.

I stopped looking at old photos, stopped listening to the songs my parents and I loved, stopped going to the places that were once our favourite hangout spots, stopped buying things my mom loved, stopped eating my dad's favourite evening snack and even worse, I stopped talking about my mom and dad, even at home. When someone mentioned them, I simply avoided the conversation.

Why? Because all of this caused me pain and reminded me that they were no longer with me. I started pretending that none of these things existed in my life anymore.

Initially, I felt like I was healing, but then I noticed my other family members, who were also deeply attached to my parents. They could discuss memories of them, laugh and cherish those memories, while I could not.

That was when I realised that I needed to accept this reality. I needed to accept that life had changed, but as humans, we cannot delete our history like computers can.

The more you run away from your emotional wounds, the more they will harm you. We often forget to prioritise our happiness. However, you know what? Regaining happiness is one of the greatest comebacks in life. We need to heal ourselves to grow. Recent research from Oxford University in the UK has shown that happy workers are 13 per cent more productive. This means that when you heal your emotional wounds, it can also enhance your productivity.

If you are struggling with any emotional wounds, I encourage you to answer the following questions with 'yes' or 'no'.

- Have you lost someone close?
- Have you ever had a heartbreak?
- Has someone insulted you in public?
- Have you faced biases (someone picking someone else over you despite you being better)?
- Has someone abandoned you?
- Have you ever cried while locked inside a room and pretended you were okay?
- Are there some topics you avoid discussing just because they hurt you?

If any of your answers is 'yes', you have identified your emotional wound.

Accept and acknowledge that, yes, it hurts. But trust me, it will not hurt forever.

P.S.: If you feel the need to consult a therapist or seek professional help at this point, go for it.

Expressing our emotions in healthy ways is crucial for releasing pent-up feelings and processing emotional pain. It is similar to a balloon filled with air without limits, and it will burst! Our emotions are like that balloon – if we bottle them up inside, they will build up, overwhelm us and ultimately break us.

What we need to do is find ways to express our emotions in a safe and healthy manner. It is like finding the perfect valve to release some air from that balloon.

One effective way to do this is through journaling. Writing down your thoughts and feelings can help you process your emotions and gain clarity about what is happening in your mind. If you enjoy art or music, you might find that expressing yourself through drawing, painting or playing an instrument can also be incredibly therapeutic. It is a way to transform your emotions into something beautiful and meaningful.

I journal every single day. It serves as my therapy, and that is why I am asking you to write answers to the questions in this book. By the end of the book, you will understand why!

Additionally, talking to someone you trust, like a friend, a life coach like me or a therapist, can make a world of difference. Sharing the weight of your emotions with someone who cares about you can offer support and perspective, helping you through tough times.

The key here is to find what works best for you. Whatever outlet you choose, the goal is to release that pent-up energy and gain a better understanding of your thoughts and feelings.

Apart from this, practising self-compassion also helps in healing emotional wounds. Self-compassion is like giving yourself a warm hug when you are feeling down.

It involves treating yourself with kindness, understanding and acceptance, especially during difficult times. Just as you would comfort a friend going through a tough situation, self-compassion means offering that same level of care and support to yourself. It is also about recognising that you are only human and that everyone makes mistakes or faces challenges at some point. Instead of being hard on yourself or criticising every move you make, self-compassion encourages you to be gentle, stop blaming yourself for what happened and practise forgiveness towards yourself.

So what can be done?

- Offer yourself words of encouragement and support during challenging times.
- Allow yourself to take breaks and rest when needed, honouring your body's signals.
- Set and respect boundaries to prioritise your well-being and needs.

- Engage in activities that bring you joy, pleasure and fulfilment.
- Practise forgiveness and let go of self-criticism for past mistakes.
- Treat yourself with the same kindness and understanding you offer to others.
- Embrace imperfection and recognise that it is part of being human.
- Practise mindfulness to stay present and aware of your thoughts and feelings.
- Focus on your strengths and celebrate your accomplishments, no matter how small.
- Surround yourself with supportive and nurturing relationships that uplift you.

Seeking support from trusted friends, family members or mental health professionals can provide validation, empathy and guidance during the healing process. Connecting with others who have experienced similar emotional wounds fosters a sense of belonging and understanding, which helps reduce feelings of isolation and shame.

Now, let me explain cognitive-behavioural techniques.

Picture this: a thought keeps recurring, like 'I am not good enough' – similar to a trending song from reels playing on loop in your mind. Cognitive restructuring focuses on challenging that thought and flipping the script.

One way to address negative thoughts is through cognitive reframing. This technique involves taking a negative thought and reshaping it to create a more positive perspective. Instead of saying, 'I am not good enough', you could reframe it as 'I am capable and worthy of success'. This practice helps you find a more balanced and empowering perspective.

Another helpful technique is thought-challenging. This approach requires you to act like a detective and investigate your thoughts. Ask yourself questions such as, 'Is this thought really true? What evidence do I have to support it?' By challenging your negative beliefs, you will begin to realise that they are not as rock-solid as they initially appeared.

Additionally, positive self-talk can be beneficial. It is like being your own cheerleader! Instead of beating yourself up, try offering words of encouragement and support. You might say, 'I have got this' or 'I am stronger than I think'.

Lastly, forgiveness is important when you are trying to heal an emotional wound.

Forgiveness is like hitting the reset button on your emotions. It means letting go of all the anger and hurt we carry around, whether directed towards ourselves or someone else.

Yes, you need to forgive yourself too. Forgive yourself for the choices you made in the past. At that time, you were a different person with a different perspective. People grow and change over time, and you should not punish yourself for evolving in life.

Many individuals feel embarrassed about their past mistakes, actions and behaviours. They often wonder why they did what they did. But remember, you were a different person back then. We grow and change with each passing moment. Just as butterflies do not look back at their caterpillar stage with shame, you should stop viewing your past with regret. It was a transformation that led to where you are now.

Forgive yourself. You deserve forgiveness.

When we forgive, it feels like we are releasing a heavy weight we have been carrying on our shoulders. Forgiveness is not about saying that what happened was okay; rather, it is about freeing ourselves from the pain and bitterness holding us back.

Forgiveness allows us to move forward without being weighed down by the past. It helps us find peace within ourselves and let go of negativity. When you feel burdened by anger or resentment, remember that forgiveness is the key to setting yourself free.

You cannot change what happened in your past, but you can choose not to be affected by it.

Along with accepting, acknowledging and practising self-compassion and forgiveness, it is also important to embrace our authenticity. Embracing vulnerability and authenticity is like opening your heart to deeper connections. It involves being real and honest about who we are, flaws and all.

When we embrace vulnerability, we essentially say, 'Hey, this is me, and I am okay with it.' This openness allows us to build trust and intimacy with ourselves and others because we no longer hide behind a facade.

If you feel like crying, go ahead and cry.

There is nothing wrong with crying. Allow yourself to cry every day and every night until you feel empty and it no longer bothers you. Many people think crying is a sign of weakness. No! Crying is simply a way to release your pain, and this is not just a theory or philosophy but a scientifically proven fact.

Research has shown that when you cry, your body releases endorphins and oxytocin, which are feel-good hormones. These natural chemical messengers help relieve emotional distress and physical pain, reduce stress and promote healing.

Ignoring emotional wounds can hinder your personal growth and well-being and it can also be detrimental to your professional life. This buildup can contribute to conditions like depression, anxiety and PTSD.

You must have heard of Dwayne 'The Rock' Johnson, the renowned actor, producer and former professional wrestler.

In the early 2000s, Dwayne Johnson faced a series of challenges in his life and career that led him into a deep state of depression. Despite his success as a professional wrestler in WWE, he felt unfulfilled and dissatisfied with the direction his life was taking. Additionally, he experienced personal difficulties, including the end of his marriage and financial struggles.

During this difficult period, Johnson found himself grappling with feelings of inadequacy, failure and hopelessness. He openly acknowledged his battle with depression, admitting that there were times when he felt 'utterly defeated' and uncertain about how to move forward.

Heal Emotional Wounds

Despite his challenges, Dwayne Johnson refused to give in to despair. He made a conscious decision to confront his demons and take control of his life, committing himself to healing his emotional wounds. Drawing on his innate resilience and determination, he embarked on a journey of self-discovery and reinvention.

A pivotal moment in this journey came when Johnson decided to transition from professional wrestling to acting. Despite facing scepticism and uncertainty from industry insiders, he remained steadfast in his pursuit of success. His breakout role in *The Scorpion King* (his second movie, released in 2002) marked the beginning of a remarkable transformation that would catapult him to Hollywood stardom. Johnson became known for his charismatic persona, larger-than-life presence and unparalleled work ethic, earning the admiration and respect of audiences worldwide.

Throughout his journey, Dwayne Johnson has been open about his struggles with depression and the importance of mental health awareness. In a 2023 interview on *The Pivot*, Johnson revealed that his mental health challenges began years ago, although he often lacked the words to express his feelings. 'I have worked hard over the years to gain the emotional tools to work through any mental pain that may come to test me,' he said.

He has candidly shared his experiences, encouraging others to seek help and break the stigma surrounding mental illness.

Johnson emphasises the importance of resilience, positivity and gratitude in overcoming adversity and achieving one's dreams.

Today, Dwayne 'The Rock' Johnson demonstrates that strength and perseverance can change your life. His journey from feeling deeply sad and dealing with several emotional wounds to becoming super successful serves as an inspiration to many.

Emotional wounds can be like persistent noises that distract us from growing and becoming our best selves.

Carrying around pain from the past is similar to having a constant buzzing in our heads, making it difficult to focus on moving forward. Healing those wounds involves quieting that noise, allowing us to clear our minds and focus on personal growth and happiness. It is about breaking free from the burdens that hold us back so we can thrive and reach our full potential.

Affirmations to Heal Emotional Wounds

- I am good and can feel better.
- I let go of bad feelings and welcome peace.
- I forgive myself and others for mistakes.
- I know I can get stronger and better every day.
- I deserve to be happy and feel calm.
- I accept my feelings and will heal.
- I face problems and find ways to fix them.
- I am kind to myself as I heal.
- I have love and help when things are hard.
- I trust I can and I will.

Inspiring Quotes

Out of suffering have emerged the strongest souls; the most massive characters are seared with scars.

— Kahlil Gibran

The wound is the place where the light enters you.

— Rumi

You say you're 'depressed' – all I see is resilience. You are allowed to feel messed up and inside out. It doesn't mean you're defective – it just means you're human.

— David Mitchell

Just when the caterpillar thought the world was over, it became a butterfly.

— Chuang Tzu

8

Rewire Your Brain for Optimism

'Life is 10 per cent what happens to you and 90 per cent how you react.' This quote by Charles Swindoll emphasises the importance of rewiring our brains for optimism because it ultimately comes down to our reactions.

Suppose you find yourself in an argument and the other person suddenly starts swearing at you in a language you do not understand. It will not affect you as intensely as if they were using a language you are familiar with. Since you do not know the words, your brain does not respond to the insults and the negativity does not impact you.

The way we react to anything and everything originates in our brain. If we do not allow something to reach our brain, it will not affect us.

Think of your brain as a super-smart computer. When you continuously think about something or focus on it, you are essentially programming that computer with specific instructions.

Imagine yourself constantly thinking, 'I am going to do great on that test' or 'I am going to get that job'. Over time, your brain begins to believe those positive thoughts because it hears them repeatedly; it is similar to training your brain to expect success.

Now, here is where it gets interesting: your brain does not just sit idly by. It actively starts looking for ways to turn those thoughts into reality! It is like a detective searching for clues to help you achieve what you are envisioning.

Have you ever noticed how some people always get lucky and achieve what they want? It is not magic or pure chance – it is science! Let me break it down for you.

Rewire Your Brain for Optimism

Our brains are like super-smart computers. They can change based on what we think and do. This ability is called neuroplasticity. It means our brains can rewire themselves to match our thoughts and experiences.

Every brain has a filter called the reticular activating system (RAS). Think of it as a bouncer at a party, allowing in only what is important to you. When you focus on a goal, a dream or even your fears and doubts, your RAS becomes attentive and helps you notice opportunities related to that focus. The RAS does not just filter sounds; it pays attention to everything you are focused on. For example, when you start thinking about buying a red car, you begin to notice red cars everywhere. That is your RAS at work, helping you recognise what is important to you.

There is a phenomenon known as confirmation bias. It can be described as a shortcut that our brains tend to favour. It seeks out evidence that supports our existing beliefs. For example, when we believe that good things will happen, our brain searches for signs reinforcing this positive expectation. But there is a catch. This process is not limited to just positive beliefs; it applies to all kinds of noises. Our brain does not distinguish between positive and negative; it merely amplifies whatever we focus on. Essentially, the principle guiding the brain is this: wherever attention goes, wherever energy flows, that particular thought or belief grows. This principle reflects a fundamental law of the universe.

The universe works in alignment with our brain on different levels: conscious, subconscious and unconscious.

Thoughts are accompanied by feelings. When you have positive thoughts, your brain releases happy chemicals like dopamine and serotonin, which make you feel good and motivate you to keep going. On the other hand, negative thoughts can trigger the release of stress hormones like cortisol and adrenaline, leading to anxiety, stress or even depression.

In a previous chapter, I explained that our brains are biased towards negative thoughts. This means that negative thinking can create a cycle where your brain focuses more on what is wrong, causing you to feel worse. It is like a downward spiral that negatively impacts your mood, motivation and overall well-being.

Your thoughts are like a roadmap, but you must drive the car. Every step you take can shape your future.

So how can we rewire our brains? Let me share what works best!

Silent Hour Rule

The 'Silent Hour' is a concept introduced by Napoleon Hill, author of *Think and Grow Rich*. He is perhaps one of the most renowned authors in the history of literature and my personal favourite. The idea behind the Silent Hour is simple yet powerful.

In our busy lives, we are constantly surrounded by noise – both internal and external. Our minds are often filled with chatter, worries and to-do lists. The Silent Hour is a dedicated time each day when you intentionally create a peaceful, quiet space for yourself.

Here is how it works:

- **Choose a time**: The Silent Hour can be at any time of the day that suits you best. It might be in the morning before the day's hustle and bustle begin, during a quiet moment in the afternoon or in the evening as a way to relax or before bedtime.
- **Find a quiet space**: Seek out a quiet and comfortable space where you will not be interrupted. This could be a cosy corner in your home, a peaceful spot in nature or even just a quiet room with the door closed.
- **Disconnect**: During your Silent Hour, disconnect from all distractions. Turn off your phone, step away from your computer and find a way to calm the external noise around you.
- **Reflect, meditate or journal**: Use this time for reflection, introspection, meditation or journaling. Sit quietly and focus on your breath, allowing your mind to settle and find calmness. Use this time to reflect on your goals, dreams and aspirations. Visualise what you want to achieve and consider how to make it happen. Write down your thoughts in your

diary or journal.
- **Practise gratitude**: Take a moment to appreciate the blessings in your life and cultivate a sense of gratitude. Reflect on what you are thankful for, big and small, and allow yourself to feel that gratitude.
- **Set intentions**: Use the Silent Hour to set intentions for the day ahead and clarify your goals and priorities. What do you want to accomplish? How do you want to show up in the world? Setting clear intentions can help guide your actions and focus your energy.
- **Stay consistent**: Consistency is the key to reaping the benefits of the Silent Hour. Try to make it a daily practice, even if it is just for a few minutes at first. Over time, you will likely notice improvements in your focus, mental clarity and overall sense of well-being.

The Silent Hour is a powerful tool for self-care, personal growth and inner peace. It is a way of practising mindfulness, which we explore in greater depth later in this book.

You can choose to have your Silent Hour at any time of the day. Personally, I prefer to do it at night when it is calm and everyone else is asleep. However, if you are an early riser, I recommend dedicating this time in the morning or whenever you feel you can be alone with yourself.

By setting aside this sacred time each day, you can cultivate a deeper connection with yourself, tap into your inner wisdom and align your actions with your highest aspirations.

Journaling

Journaling is a simple yet incredibly powerful tool for rewiring your brain for optimism and quieting the noises of your life.

You may have heard about journaling before, perhaps you have even tried it a few times, but let us explore what journaling really is and how it can transform your life.

So what exactly is journaling?

At its core, journaling is the practice of writing down your thoughts, feelings, experiences and ideas, whether on paper or digitally. It is akin to having a conversation with yourself, a trusted friend or even the universe. It provides a safe space where you can freely express your heart and mind without fear of judgement.

Journaling is a powerful tool for self-discovery and self-awareness, helping you gain clarity in life, whether it is about your noises or goals.

When you take the time to put pen to paper and express your thoughts and emotions, you gain insights into yourself that you might not have recognised otherwise. You begin to identify patterns in your thinking, recognise recurring emotions and gain clarity about what truly matters to you.

Journaling is incredibly therapeutic – it is like a form of therapy on paper. When you write about your noises, challenges, fears and anxieties, you release them from the confines of your mind and onto the page. This act can feel like lifting a weight off your shoulders. As you write, you may find that solutions arise, insights emerge, and you feel lighter and more at peace.

Another incredible benefit of journaling is that it allows you to track your progress and growth over time. By looking back on old journal entries, you can see how far you have come, what you have learned and how you have overcome obstacles. This reflection serves as a powerful reminder of your resilience and strength.

One of the most profound benefits of journaling is that it deepens your relationship with yourself and facilitates healing. When you commit to journaling regularly, you are essentially making a commitment to yourself. You say, 'I value my thoughts, feelings and experiences enough to give them the space and attention they deserve.' In doing so, you strengthen your self-trust, self-love and self-compassion.

You may be thinking, 'That sounds great, but how do I actually start journaling?'

Well, the beauty of journaling is that there are no strict rules.

You can make it whatever you want it to be. But if you are looking for some guidance, here are a few tips to get you started:

- **Find the right tools**: Choose a journal or notebook that resonates with you. It could be a fancy leather-bound journal, a simple spiral notebook or even a digital journaling app – whatever feels comfortable and inspiring to you.
- **Set aside time**: Find a time in your day when you can set aside a few minutes for journaling. This could be in the morning, before bed or during your lunch break. The important thing is to make it a regular part of your routine.
- **Write freely**: Remember, there are no rules when it comes to journaling. Write whatever comes to mind without censoring yourself or worrying about grammar and punctuation. Let your thoughts flow freely onto the page.
- **Experiment with prompts**: If you are not sure what to write, try using prompts to get your creative juices flowing. You can find journaling prompts online or in books or you can simply ask yourself questions like, 'How am I feeling today?' or 'What am I grateful for?'
- **Be consistent**: Like any habit, journaling is most effective when done consistently. Try to make it a daily practice, even if it is just for a few minutes each day. The more you journal, the more benefits you will experience.

In order to rewire your brain for optimism and shoo away the noises, you can simply begin by writing affirmations.

Affirmations are positive statements you repeat yourself regularly, aiming to change your beliefs, thoughts and behaviours. They act like little seeds of positivity that you plant in your mind, nurturing them until they become powerful catalysts for change.

Affirmations are like pep talks we give ourselves to boost our spirits and change our mindset.

Our brains are like clay, always moulding and changing. Remember neuroplasticity, which I mentioned in a previous chapter? It refers to the brain's ability to rewire itself based on our experiences and habits. Additionally, the RAS is also activated when we start using affirmations.

When we repeat affirmations, we are essentially providing our brains with a new script to follow. We tell ourselves positive statements like 'I am strong', 'I am worthy' or 'I am capable'. And guess what? Our brains start to believe it!

There are many ways to work with affirmations. I personally love to journal affirmations, but apart from this, you can sing, chant, listen to or even read affirmations to reap the benefits.

Journaling has become a habit for me now. I currently maintain at least five journals simultaneously: a gratitude journal, a dump journal, a daily journal, a work journal and an anger management journal. I typically journal in the morning and often at night before going to bed. I especially focus on night journaling when I have had a bad day. In these entries, I express all my negativity, doubts, anger and thoughts, allowing me to sleep with a lighter heart.

Many well-known personalities like Nelson Mandela, Robin Sharma, Serena Williams, Oprah Winfrey, Jennifer Aniston, Lady Gaga and Warren Buffett also practise journaling every day.

In addition to affirmations, you can write anything you wish in your journal – there are absolutely no rules. You do not have to rely on journaling prompts to guide your writing.

No! Pour your heart out. If you are happy, journal it. If you are sad or angry, journal it. If you have a dream, journal it. If you face a failure, journal it. If you had a fight, journal it. If you feel guilty, journal it.

The idea is to simply clear your mind of heavy thoughts, especially the ones you do not share with anyone. This practice helps release negativity from your energy system, allowing more room for positivity, clarity and personal growth.

Meditation

Meditation is a practice that trains your mind to focus and be present in the moment. It is like giving your brain a workout. But instead of lifting weights, you are strengthening your ability to be aware of your thoughts and emotions without becoming overwhelmed by them.

When people hear the term 'meditation', they often picture someone sitting peacefully amid nature or in a vast, quiet room, lost in contemplation for hours.

While this may be true for some, it is not a mandatory method of meditation. Deepak Chopra says, 'The goal of meditation is not to control your thoughts. It is to stop letting them control you.' So the goal of meditation is not to stop your thoughts or clear your mind completely (which can be pretty tough, let us be honest!) but rather to cultivate a sense of awareness and acceptance of whatever arises in your mind and body.

There are many different types of meditation, but one of the most common techniques is mindfulness meditation.

In mindfulness meditation, you simply observe your thoughts, sensations and emotions as they arise, without judgement or attachment. You might focus on your breath, bodily sensations or even the sounds around you.

If you have never meditated before and have a short attention span or anxiety issues, it can initially be a little difficult to practise.

For someone new to meditation, here are some tips to get started (this is how I began, and it helped me):

- **Start small**: You do not have to meditate for hours immediately. Begin with just a few minutes each day and gradually increase the duration as you feel more comfortable.
- **Find a quiet space**: Choose a quiet, comfortable space where you will not be disturbed. It could be your bedroom, a cosy corner of your home or even a park if you prefer being outdoors.

- **Focus on your breath**: Close your eyes and focus on your breath. Pay attention to the sensation of air entering and leaving your body. When your mind starts to wander (which it will!), gently bring your focus back to your breath. While doing this, you can also chant 'OM' or any mantra or any master switchword in your mind.
- **Be patient and kind to yourself**: Meditation is a practice that takes time and patience to master. Do not be discouraged if your mind feels busy or restless at first – just keep returning to your breath. Remember, it is called a meditation practice for a reason!

If you're feeling overwhelmed and thinking, 'I cannot do this!', then let me offer you another option.

But first, let me share a little secret with you.

I do not meditate every day. A few years ago, I used to meditate every morning, but now my routine has changed. Instead, I have adopted other techniques to rewire my brain and shoo away the noises around me, such as journaling, praying and practising the laws of the universe. However, there is still one practice I use consistently.

This is one of my hacks. When I feel mentally cluttered and the weight of the world is bearing down on me, I meditate to help me sleep.

There are many free meditation audios and music available online. See, every coin has two sides. So the internet is not just a noise but also a boon in many ways.

I control how I use the internet. I make it useful to me. While we cannot avoid technology, we can surely use it wisely.

I put on my earphones, play a meditation audio and drift off to sleep. Many times, I just use the speaker on my phone, lower the volume so that only I can hear it and keep it beside my pillow or on my bedside table. The best part about these meditation audios is the variety available. From guided meditations to rain sounds, flute music, piano melodies, nature sounds, jungle ambience, singing bowl tones and subliminals – there is something for everyone.

So if you cannot find the time to sit down and meditate, I highly recommend trying guided meditation audios or calming music. Trust me, you will want to reach out to me on Facebook or Instagram to thank me later!

Physical Activity

When I say 'physical activity', I do not mean you must hit the gym starting tomorrow. While that is a great option, what I mean by 'physical activity' includes any activity that gets your body moving and your heart pumping.

Think about activities like dancing, swimming, hiking, playing sports or even just taking a brisk walk around the neighbourhood.

So why is physical activity such a game-changer in rewiring our brains for optimism and helping us shoo the noises?

Let us start by discussing the remarkable chemicals called endorphins. When we engage in physical activities like jogging, dancing or yoga, our brains release these feel-good neurotransmitters that bring happiness and joy to our bodies. It is as if we are experiencing our own personal dose of sunshine on a cloudy day! These endorphins not only enhance our mood in the moment but also have lasting effects on our overall outlook on life.

But that is not all! Physical activity is also a powerhouse when it comes to kicking stress to the curb. When we engage in physical activity, our bodies release tension and stress, leaving us feeling calm, centred and ready to take on whatever life throws our way. It is like hitting the reset button on our stress levels, giving us a fresh perspective and a renewed sense of optimism.

Additionally, physical activity helps improve brain function. When we exercise, blood flow to the brain increases, delivering oxygen and nutrients that keep our grey matter in excellent condition. This boost in blood flow not only improves cognitive function and memory but also helps us think more clearly and creatively. It is akin to giving our brains a much-needed spa day, leaving us feeling refreshed, rejuvenated and ready to tackle any challenges that come our way.

Perhaps the most powerful aspect of physical activity is its ability to build resilience and foster a sense of empowerment. When we set fitness goals and work hard to achieve them, we prove to ourselves that we are capable of more than we ever imagined. Each little victory, whether it is running a mile without stopping or mastering a new yoga pose, reminds us of our strength and resilience. It is like flexing our mental muscles and demonstrating to the world (and ourselves!) what we are made of.

It is a myth that physical activity is solely about breaking a sweat and burning calories (though those are nice benefits!). It is also about nourishing our bodies, calming our minds and empowering ourselves to live our best lives.

You might be wondering, 'What kind of physical activities should I try?' The options are endless! Here are a few ideas to help you get started:

- **Walking**: It is simple, free and something we can do just about anywhere! Take a stroll around your neighbourhood, explore a nearby park or go for a scenic hike in nature. Walking is a great way to clear your mind, get some fresh air and soak up the beauty of the world around you.
- **Yoga**: Yoga not only improves flexibility, strength and balance but is also a powerful tool for calming the mind and reducing stress. Whether you are a seasoned yogi or a total newbie, there is a yoga practice out there for everyone. Roll out your mat, strike a pose and let the zen vibes flow!
- **Swimming**: Dive into the deep end and make a splash with some swimming! Not only is it a great full-body workout, but it is also gentle on the joints and perfect for all fitness levels. Whether you are doing laps in the pool or frolicking in the ocean waves, swimming is a refreshing way to get your heart pumping and cool off on a hot day.

- **Team sports**: Put on your game face and join a team sport like football, basketball or volleyball. It is a great way to stay active and improve your skills. Plus, it offers a fantastic opportunity to bond with teammates, learn the value of teamwork and unleash your competitive spirit.
- **Cycling**: Hit the open road (or the stationary bike at the gym) and pedal your way to fitness! Cycling is a low-impact exercise that is easy on the joints and great for cardiovascular health. Whether cruising along scenic trails or tackling challenging terrain, cycling is a fun and exhilarating way to explore the great outdoors and get your heart pumping.
- **Dancing**: Who says physical activity has to be boring? Turn up your favourite tunes and let loose on the dance floor (or in your living room!). Whether you are busting out your best moves or grooving to the beat, dancing is a fun and joyful way to get your body moving and lift your spirits. This one is my personal favourite, and I do it almost every single day!

Praying

It does not matter if you believe in God or not, nor does it matter which religion you follow or where you come from – praying is indeed one of the most powerful tools for rewiring your brain.

Praying is something I do every single day, morning and night. In fact, even during the daytime, when I feel lost and low, I pray. I believe that praying is a conversation with something greater than ourselves. It is like reaching out to the universe, a higher power or whatever you believe in and sharing your thoughts, hopes and wishes.

Philosophers have various perspectives on prayer. Some view it as a way to connect with the divine, while others see it as a form of reflection and introspection.

Consider prayer a moment of pause amid the hustle and bustle of life. It provides a chance to step back, take a deep breath and reflect on the big questions: Who am I? What do I value? What do I really want?

When we pray, we are not just asking for things (although that is part of it!). We also express gratitude for the good things in our lives and seek guidance when things get tough. It is like having a heartfelt conversation with the universe or the divine, trusting that our words are heard and understood.

Some philosophers argue that prayer is just about talking, but I believe it is also about listening. It involves being open to receiving insights, inspiration and answers from the universe. It is like tuning in to a cosmic radio station and being receptive to the messages being broadcast. I refer to these insights as 'downloads' from the divine.

When I was on the verge of giving up everything, it was prayer that saved me. There is faith that comes from knowing someone above is listening and will surely send help when needed.

Praying is not a one-size-fits-all practice. It is deeply personal and unique to each individual. Some people pray through rituals and ceremonies, while others prefer quiet contemplation or spontaneous conversations. You can create your own rules because there are no rules for praying. While every religion offers some guidelines for prayer, I believe that when you seek guidance from the divine from the depths of your heart and soul, the divine responds. I have my own set of rules for praying. It is a personal thing between me and my God. It should be the same for you – it should be between you and your God or the universe or angels, whoever you believe in.

Whether you pray to God, the universe or simply to your inner wisdom, remember that you are not just asking for help but also opening your mind to receive insights. These insights, which can come in the form of signs, intuitions or serendipities, are often your solutions.

It is important to pray not only during difficult times but also in moments of joy. Express gratitude for everything around you because the more gratitude you express for a particular thing, the more it will come your way.

When we pray, we are entrusting our lives to a higher power. Praying with complete faith signals to our subconscious mind that things will be resolved. This positive mindset enables your brain to focus on solutions rather than obstacles. Making prayer a daily habit can gradually shift your thought patterns, helping you rewire your brain and quiet the noises that block your path to growth.

Music

Music has an incredible power to evoke a wide range of emotions. Have you ever listened to a song that instantly lifted your mood or brought tears to your eyes? This happens because music has a direct connection to our brains and emotions.

When we listen to music we love, our brains release dopamine, a natural happy pill. This is the same chemical released when we eat delicious food or fall in love. Similarly, when we listen to sad music, our brains release different chemicals and hormones. One of these is prolactin, often associated with crying and emotional release. Now you understand why music can make you feel happy or sad!

Music does not just influence our emotions – it also has a profound impact on our brains. When we listen to music, different areas of our brain light up like fireworks, including those responsible for memory, language and even motor skills.

Studies have shown that music can actually rewire our brains for the better. Surprising but true!

This is why it is important to choose carefully the kind of music we listen to. For instance, if you are feeling stressed or anxious, soothing instrumental music can help calm your nerves and bring you back to a centred state. On the other hand, if you want to boost your energy and motivation, upbeat, uplifting tunes are the way to go!

It is not just about the genre of music – it is also about how it makes you feel. If a certain song brings back bad memories or leaves you feeling down, it is perfectly okay to skip it and find something that lifts your spirits instead. This is mainly because when you listen to songs with negative lyrics – like 'I am so lonely, I have nobody' and 'My life's a mess' – and play them on a loop, you may inadvertently affirm those negative feelings. Your brain does not distinguish between listening for entertainment and using those lyrics as a chant or prayer; it simply reacts to how you feel. The chemicals in your brain will respond accordingly, ultimately attracting more negativity into your life.

Whether you are jamming out to your favourite playlist or discovering new tunes that speak to your soul, remember that music is not just background noise – it is a powerful force that can shape our brains, lift our spirits and help us grow into the best versions of ourselves.

The next time you listen to a song, focus on the lyrics. If the message is something you do not want in your life, skip it and tune into something more positive and uplifting.

Celebrate Small Wins

A young man named Dhruv, an Indian boy whose startup had failed just six months after its launch, approached Monk Aishi, who lived in the Key Gompa in Ladakh.

Dhruv's face was etched with disappointment and despair. Having lost all his savings to the failed startup, he felt overwhelmed and wanted to give up on life.

'Brother Aishi,' Dhruv began, his voice heavy with emotion, 'I have come seeking guidance. I have worked so hard to achieve my goals, but despite my efforts, I have fallen short. I feel like giving up. I have failed, and I do not believe I can ever be successful. I do not have the money or courage to start over.'

Brother Aishi smiled, his gaze warm and compassionate. 'Sit with me, Dhruv,' he said, patting the ground beside him. 'Let us talk.' Dhruv settled next to Brother Aishi, his heart heavy with the weight of his burdens. 'I thought success was within my reach,' he confessed, his voice trembling. 'But now, I do not know what to do. I cannot ask my parents for money, and I cannot even face the investors. It was a big opportunity, and I failed terribly.'

Brother Aishi nodded knowingly. 'Success is not measured by the absence of failure, Dhruv,' he said gently. 'It is defined by our response to adversity and our resilience in the face of challenges.'

'What was your goal when you launched your startup?' asked Brother Aishi.

'I wanted it to become a unicorn,' Dhruv replied, 'which means a startup company with a value of over $1 billion.'

'And then what did you do every day?'

'I was following everything necessary to become successful in life. I worked hard and smart, day and night. I also meditated, journalled, prayed and practised manifestation. I visualised my company turning into a unicorn every single day. I woke up with the mindset that my company would become a unicorn. I do not know what went wrong or where I failed.'

'Everything was right, except for one thing,' smiled Brother Aishi. 'Your goal. You need to have a clear vision of where you want to go, but when it comes to your daily tasks, you should set small, achievable goals and celebrate those wins every day.'

Dhruv listened as Brother Aishi continued to explain, 'I am sure you have not climbed Mount Everest, but let me share something interesting. Have you ever wondered why it has several campsites?'

'To provide climbers with a place to rest and recharge for the journey ahead?'

'Correct. But there is more to it. When you actually climb a mountain, you have a destination in mind, but when you begin your journey, you set a goal to reach the next campsite. Each morning, you wake up with the target of reaching the next campsite. Once you arrive, you can retire for the day, feeling content and happy that you have accomplished your goal.'

'Yes!'

'If you think about climbing a mountain that is 8,848.86 m high, it can make you anxious, restless and feel immense pressure. However, if you tell your brain that you need to cover 20 km today, your mind will support you in achieving that,' Brother Aishi explained. 'You need to set small goals and celebrate small wins every day.'

Brother Aishi smiled kindly. 'Success is not a destination; it is a journey marked by small victories and moments of courage and perseverance.'

He gestured towards the lush greenery surrounding them. 'Just as the mighty oak tree grows from a tiny seed, success also emerges from the humblest of beginnings. It is in the small, everyday triumphs that we find the seeds of greatness.'

'Small wins are the stepping stones that lead us towards our goals. They represent the little victories we achieve each day – the moments of progress, growth and achievement that may seem insignificant on their own but collectively propel us forward on our path,' Brother Aishi explained.

Dhruv nodded in understanding, beginning to realise that even the smallest triumphs can hold great significance.

'But how can I find success after such a defeat?' Dhruv asked, his voice filled with uncertainty.

'Failure is not the end of the road, Dhruv,' Brother Aishi replied. 'Failure is merely a detour – a chance to learn, to grow and to uncover new strengths within ourselves.'

Like Dhruv, we all need to understand the importance of starting small. While it is essential to have a clear vision of our destination, these pit stops along the way are equally important.

As we celebrate these small wins, we cultivate a mindset of gratitude, resilience and growth. We acknowledge our progress, no matter how small and build momentum towards our larger goals. Our brain switches to the success mindset with these small wins. It is like making your brain accustomed to winning. Once your brain develops a success mindset, it starts to deliver world-class performance at your highest potential.

When I write a book, I typically set a target of around 60,000 words for the entire manuscript. However, when I actually sit down to write, I set small targets, like 5,000 words a day. Sometimes I win, and sometimes I fail, but I do not stop because I know that every single effort counts.

You need to prepare yourself and train your brain to feel happy and proud of yourself by at least taking a small step and achieving it.

Seven Best Practices to Celebrate Small Wins

- Set small goals and try to achieve them by the end of the day.
- Cultivate gratitude for the progress you have made, irrespective of its size.
- Treat yourself to a small reward as an acknowledgement of your achievements. For instance, I reward myself with ice cream or a movie when I accomplish a small goal. I control myself until I have done it.
- Share your successes with loved ones, letting them partake in your happiness. When I accomplish a small win, I order ice cream for everyone in my house. This induces positivity in my personal win, fuelling my brain to achieve the next goal.
- Keep a journal to document, track and appreciate your daily wins.
- Be kind to yourself. If you fail, try again.
- Remind yourself that small steps are paving the way to your ultimate future.

Forgiveness

Forgiveness is like sunshine after a storm – it has the power to illuminate our darkest moments and pave the way for new beginnings.

You might wonder how this is relevant here.

Everything is interconnected.

Forgiveness is not just about letting go of past hurts – it is about reclaiming our power, healing our hearts and embracing a future filled with hope and possibility. When we forgive, we release the heavy burden of resentment and bitterness that weighs us down, allowing us to move forward with grace and resilience.

As we have seen throughout this book, emotional wounds, regrets and grudges can create the biggest noises in our lives, hindering our growth and success.

Think about when someone wronged you, hurt you deeply or betrayed your trust. It is easy to cling to grudges and allow anger and resentment to fester in our hearts like toxic weeds. However, when we hold onto anger, we are only hurting ourselves. As the saying goes, 'Holding onto anger is like drinking poison and expecting the other person to die.'

Forgiving others is not about excusing their behaviour or pretending that the hurt never happened. Instead, it is about acknowledging the pain, choosing compassion over bitterness and refusing to let past wounds define our present and future. When we forgive, we reclaim our power and set ourselves free from the chains of resentment.

And not just others. We often become cruel to ourselves as well. Tell me, how often have we beaten ourselves up over past mistakes, failures or shortcomings?

It is all too easy to get caught in a cycle of self-blame and self-criticism, allowing the voice of our inner critic to drown out the gentler whispers of self-compassion.

Here is the truth: we are all human. We are bound to make mistakes, stumble and fall along the way. Forgiving ourselves is not about pretending that our mistakes did not happen – it is about embracing our humanity, learning from our experiences and extending the same compassion to ourselves that we would to a dear friend.

But how does forgiveness rewire our brains?

Let us talk science!

When we hold onto anger and resentment, our brains become stuck in a negative feedback loop. We become hyper-focused on past hurts, replaying painful memories over and over again like a broken record.

But when we choose to forgive, something remarkable occurs in our brains. Neuroscientists have discovered that forgiveness activates areas associated with empathy, compassion and emotional regulation. It literally rewires our neural pathways, shifting our focus from negativity to positivity, from pain to healing.

Practising forgiveness creates space for personal growth, creativity and innovation to thrive. We release the burdens of the past and embrace the present, allowing ourselves to fully engage with the opportunities and possibilities that await us.

Moreover, forgiveness is a powerful tool for building meaningful relationships, fostering trust and cultivating a positive work environment.

As leaders, entrepreneurs and change-makers, our ability to forgive and extend grace to others sets the tone for our organisations and communities, inspiring others to follow suit and create a culture of empathy and understanding.

Forgiveness is not a one-time event – it is a journey, a practice and a way of life. It is about choosing love over hate, compassion over judgement and resilience over despair.

Holding on to a grudge is like filling your energy system with dirt and pollution, both for yourself and for others. To make space for growth and joy, you must cleanse your energy system.

Travel

Travel serves as a reset button for your brain, bringing back a fresh dose of optimism.

Imagine standing atop a majestic mountain, the crisp air filling your lungs as you gaze at a breathtaking vista. That sense of awe and wonder washing over you? That is the magic of travel – rewiring your brain for a more positive outlook.

This is not just feel-good talk; it is scientifically proven. Studies have shown that travel can have a profound impact on our mental and emotional well-being. And you will be surprised to know that even the anticipation of a trip can boost happiness levels. Our brains release dopamine – the feel-good hormone – when we have something exciting to look forward to. Once we embark on our journey, the novelty and adventure of travel stimulate the brain's reward centres, leading to increased feelings of happiness and optimism.

Travel promotes neuroplasticity, the brain's ability to reorganise and form new neural connections. As mentioned earlier in this book, when we encounter new experiences, sights and sounds, our brains become highly active, creating pathways that enhance cognitive function and emotional resilience. In other words, travel literally rewires our brains for optimism by exposing us to new perspectives and challenges that push us out of our comfort zones.

Stepping out of your comfort zone is a crucial aspect of travel. When you travel, you experience the unknown firsthand. Whether it is trying new foods, navigating unfamiliar streets or communicating in a different language, each day of your trip becomes an adventure. And you know what? This is beneficial for your brain! It is like giving your neurons a workout, challenging them to adapt and grow in new ways.

Additionally, travelling allows you to see the world through a different lens. Suddenly, your problems and worries appear smaller in the grand scheme of things. You begin to realise there is a vast world out there, filled with beauty and wonder. This shift in perspective can significantly improve your mood and overall outlook on life.

But wait, there is more!

Travelling serves as a crash course in resilience. You will encounter a few bumps along the way – missed flights, lost luggage, language barriers or a wrong choice of hotels – but you learn to roll with the punches and emerge stronger on the other side.

Each challenge you overcome boosts your confidence and resilience, demonstrating your ability.

And let us not forget about connections!

When you travel, you open yourself up to new people and experiences. Whether bonding with fellow travellers over shared adventures or connecting with locals who welcome you into their homes, these connections leave a lasting impact. They remind us that we are all in this together and that kindness and hospitality know no borders.

So how does this rewiring happen? Well, it is like a symphony of neurons firing and rewiring in your brain. Your brain thrives on novelty and travel is chock-full of it!

This rewiring sticks with you long after you have unpacked your bags and returned to your daily routine. Research suggests that the positive effects of travel can linger long after we have returned home. Memories of our adventures serve as a source of inspiration and motivation, reminding us of our ability to overcome obstacles and embrace new opportunities.

Moreover, the skills and qualities we develop through travel – such as adaptability, open-mindedness and resilience – continue to shape our outlook on life, making us more optimistic and hopeful for the future.

As I write this section of the book, I feel like a travel agent trying to convince you to buy a tour package from me!

But in all seriousness, travel does help a lot.

I learned this from my dad. He was a banker with a limited number of vacation days. He often said that travelling is the biggest healer, the greatest source of motivation and the best way to shoo the noises in our lives that act as a barrier to our growth.

Can you believe we used to take a trip every three to four months? I watched him plan these trips in advance, utilising his long weekends and even opting for unpaid leave when necessary. He would say that travel is the best way to spend our money. Through travel, we gain experiences that stay with us for a lifetime. It rejuvenates us, and when we return, we do so with a fresh perspective and renewed motivation.

The Indian government bank, where my dad worked, has a policy that allows its employees to take a long vacation of about six to eight days every three years, with all expenses covered for their families. In addition to this benefit, my dad funded all the trips we took from his savings.

This experience has been incredibly valuable. Everything I have shared earlier about travel is not just research-based; it is rooted in my personal experience.

And it is not just my family and me who have benefited from travel; we can also look at famous people like Chris Hemsworth, Roger Federer and Robin Sharma. They are often seen travelling – why? Because travel is one of the best ways to reset, eliminate distractions and return stronger and wiser.

When you travel, you embrace change and uncertainty with open arms, knowing that the world is full of endless adventures waiting to be discovered.

So the next time you feel stuck in a rut or weighed down by worries, why not book that plane ticket or hop on a bus for a spontaneous road trip? Trust me, your brain and soul will thank you for it.

Inspiring Quotes

The optimist proclaims that we live in the best of all possible worlds, and the pessimist fears this is true.

- James Branch Cabell

Optimism is essential to achievement and it is also the foundation of courage and true progress.

- Nicholas M. Butler

I am fundamentally an optimist. Whether that comes from nature or nurture, I cannot say. Part of being optimistic is keeping one's head pointed toward the sun, one's feet moving forward.

- Nelson Mandela

Optimism is the most important human trait, because it allows us to evolve our ideas, to improve our situation and to hope for a better tomorrow.

- Seth Godin

A pessimist sees the difficulty in every opportunity; an optimist sees the opportunity in every difficulty.

- Winston Churchill

9

Cultivate a Resilient Mindset

Think of resilience as your superpower – the ability to bounce back from life's challenges, setbacks and disappointments stronger and more determined than ever. Resilience is not about avoiding difficult situations or pretending that everything is fine when it is not. It is about facing adversity head-on, adapting to change and emerging from the storm with newfound strength and wisdom.

Cultivating a resilient mindset filters out all the noises that block your path to growth in life.

Think of your inner strength as a muscle you can strengthen and flex – a source of resilience you can draw upon whenever life throws you a curveball.

Life is full of twists and turns, with its ups and downs. Instead of resisting change, embrace it as an opportunity for growth and self-discovery. Remember that the only constant in life is change, so why not become friends with it?

We need to be kind to ourselves, especially during tough times. Treat yourself with the same kindness and understanding that you would offer to a friend in need. Remember, you are doing the best you can with the tools you have.

Cultivating a resilient mindset requires maintaining a positive outlook, even in the face of adversity. It is important to look for the silver lining in every situation, focusing on the lessons learned and the opportunities for growth that come with challenges.

Instead of getting bogged down by problems, approach them as opportunities for creative solutions. Break larger problems into smaller, more manageable steps and address them one at a time.

Stay present in the moment by fully experiencing your thoughts, feelings and sensations without judgement. Practising mindfulness helps you stay grounded and centred, even amid life's chaos.

Connect with your values and passions, and allow them to guide you through challenging times. A sense of purpose gives you direction and motivation, even when the going gets tough.

Cultivating a resilient mindset is a lifelong journey, not a destination. With resilience as our compass, there is no limit to what we can achieve. Resilience is the first step to becoming unstoppable in life, like a Porsche with no brakes.

If I had not cultivated a resilient mindset, I would not be writing this book or speaking to you.

Every great person experiences failure, but they do not give up. They focus on their comeback instead of lamenting past failures.

I follow the ABC rule to cultivate a resilient mindset.

A – Awareness

You become aware of everything about you – what works for you, what does not, your strengths, your weaknesses and everything else. This happens through practising mindfulness.

B – Well-being

When you fail and face a setback, it brings a lot of noises along – stress, anxiety, fear, doubts. It is during these times that focusing on your overall well-being, both physical and mental, becomes crucial.

C – Coping

You need to tell yourself that quitting is not an option. You must find ways and solutions to get started once again.

Find Your 'Why'

Your 'why' is your driving force, your deepest reason for doing what you do. It embodies the passion, purpose and meaning behind your actions, serving as the fuel that propels you forward, even when the going gets tough.

Understanding your 'why' is like discovering your North Star; it guides you on your journey, keeping you focused and grounded amid life's twists and turns.

Your 'why' is your anchor in stormy seas, providing you with strength and motivation during challenging times. When you are clear about your purpose and passion, you are better equipped to weather life's storms with grace and determination.

So how can you uncover your 'why' and tap into its transformative power?

- **Reflect on your passions**: Take some time to reflect on the things that light you up, the activities that make your heart sing and the causes that stir your soul. What brings you joy and fulfilment? What are you truly passionate about?
- **Identify your values**: Think about the values that matter most to you – such as integrity, compassion, creativity and justice, to name a few. Your 'why' is often deeply connected to your core values, so identifying them can provide valuable insight into your purpose.
- **Explore your past experiences**: Reflect on past experiences, both positive and negative, that have shaped who you are today. What lessons have you learned along the way? How have these experiences influenced your values and priorities?
- **Connect with your inner child**: Reflect on your childhood dreams and aspirations. What did you dream of becoming when you were younger? What activities brought you joy and excitement? Sometimes, reconnecting with your inner child can reveal valuable clues about your 'why'.

- **Listen to your intuition**: Pay attention to the subtle whispers of your heart and the nudges of your intuition. Sometimes, our deepest truths are hidden beneath the surface, waiting to be unearthed when we quiet the noise and listen to the wisdom within.
- **Remind yourself why you started**: This simple reminder can help you maintain focus and push forward, no matter what challenges come your way. When you remind yourself why you started in the first place, you can reignite your passion and purpose, helping you bounce back with even greater zeal.
- **Start afresh**: If you have a habit of maintaining a yearly journal, how does it work? Every year, you get a new journal and start filling it out one day at a time. You are aware of what happened last time, and you know what needs to be done to improve and grow. Similarly, when you face failure or a setback, you must hit that reset button and start from scratch.

Your 'why' serves as your compass, your guiding star in a world of noises. By uncovering your purpose and passion, you empower yourself to navigate life's challenges with resilience, courage and clarity. Your 'why' needs to be discovered and reinforced in your mind repeatedly; it will keep you motivated for growth and moving forward.

Gratitude Attitude

Ah, the 'gratitude attitude'! It is like putting on a pair of magical glasses that help us see the beauty and blessings around us. Having a gratitude attitude means approaching life with a heart full of appreciation and thankfulness for the little things, the big things and everything in between.

Imagine waking up each day with a smile, feeling grateful for the gift of a new day and the endless possibilities it holds. It is about pausing to admire the sunrise, feeling the warmth of the sun on your skin and taking a moment to breathe in the beauty of the world around you.

With a gratitude attitude, even the simplest moments become precious treasures to be cherished and celebrated. It is about finding joy in the ordinary, delighting in the unexpected and marvelling at the everyday miracles surrounding us.

Gratitude and resilience are closely connected, like two peas in a pod! They complement each other, creating a beautiful harmony in our lives.

Gratitude goes beyond simply saying 'thank you' when someone does something nice for us (although that is important too!). It involves recognising the beauty and blessings in our lives, big and small, and feeling genuinely thankful for them.

When we practise gratitude, we shift our focus from what we lack to what we have, moving from a mindset of scarcity to one of abundance. It is like flipping a switch in our minds, illuminating the good around us even during tough times. That is where the magic begins.

Gratitude plays a key role in building resilience and here is how:

- **Shifting Perspectives**
  When we practise gratitude, we change our perspective from focusing on what is going wrong to appreciating what is going right. We shift our attention from what we lack to what we already have. Instead of dwelling on our challenges, we focus on the blessings around us, finding joy and beauty even amid difficult times.

- **Finding Strength in Adversity**
  Practising gratitude helps us cultivate a mindset focused on abundance rather than scarcity. It makes us more resilient because we recognise that even in the toughest times, there are still reasons to be thankful. Gratitude gives us the strength to face our challenges with courage and optimism, knowing that there is goodness to be found even in the darkest moments.

- **Fostering Connection and Support**
  Gratitude strengthens our connections with others, fostering a sense of community and support. When we express

gratitude towards friends, family and loved ones, we deepen our relationships and create a network of support that helps us weather life's storms with grace and resilience. Knowing that we are not alone, that we have people who care about us and are there for us, gives us the strength to keep going even when times are tough.

One of the best ways to cultivate gratitude to build a resilient mindset is to maintain a gratitude journal.

I have been doing this every day, and I do not even remember when I started. Keeping a gratitude journal is simple yet powerful; it strengthens your focus, provides clarity and helps attract all that you want in your life.

A gratitude journal is essentially a special book where you write down things you are thankful for every day. It is a bit like collecting treasures – with each entry representing moments of joy and appreciation.

Each day, take a few minutes to jot down things you are grateful for. These can be big, like spending time with loved ones, or small, like the smell of fresh flowers or a funny joke you heard. The beauty of a gratitude journal is that it helps us notice and celebrate the good stuff in our lives, even on days when things might feel tough.

It is like planting seeds of positivity and watching them grow into beautiful flowers of gratitude. And the best part? You can look back on your journal whenever you need a little boost of happiness. It is like having a treasure trove of joy right at your fingertips.

Starting a gratitude journal is easy!

Start by writing down five things you are grateful for. You can write this at night, as it helps you reflect on your day and appreciate the small moments.

Even if life feels overwhelming or challenging, make an effort to find five things that made you smile today. These can be as simple as a forwarded text message on WhatsApp that brightened your day or a funny meme you saw on Instagram.

Another powerful way to cultivate a 'gratitude attitude' is through small acts of kindness.

When you feel helpless in life, go help someone else. This will remind you that no matter how you feel about your life and position right now, you are still in a better place than someone else.

When we help others, we start to notice all the positive aspects of our own lives as well. It is like flipping on a gratitude switch in our brains. Suddenly, we are not just focused on the negative; we start to see all the little blessings hiding in plain sight.

That is why I encourage practising a random act of kindness every day. Karma is real, and it comes back to us multiplied. Some random acts of kindness that I suggest to my mentees are as follows:

- Smile or wave at a stranger.
- Hold the door open for someone.
- Compliment a friend or co-worker.
- Send a handwritten note of appreciation to someone you care about.
- Buy an ice cream or candies for a child in need.
- Offer to help a neighbour with their groceries or garden.
- Pay for the coffee or meal of the person behind you in line.
- Give up your spot in a queue to someone at the back.
- Listen attentively to someone who needs to talk.
- Send a text message to check in on a friend or family member.
- Leave a positive review for a local business or service.
- Donate gently used clothes or household items to a charity.
- Share your favourite book or movie with a friend.
- Plant a tree or flowers in a public space.
- Offer to babysit for a friend or neighbour.
- Leave encouraging sticky notes in public places for strangers to find.
- Cook a meal or bake treats for a friend or family member.
- Offer to walk a friend's or a neighbour's dog or pet-sit for them.

- Volunteer at a local shelter, food bank or community organisation.
- Offer to drive a friend or family member to appointments or errands.
- Send a care package to someone who could use a pick-me-up.
- Simply listen without judgement when someone needs to vent or share their feelings.

On the second day of my Life Retreat in Rishikesh, I took all the participants to the marketplace and instructed them to perform at least three acts of kindness. I also asked them to record the reactions of the people they helped, as well as their own feelings, on their phones.

When everyone returned, they were all wearing huge smiles and were as excited as children, eager to share their experiences.

One sentiment was common among all their reactions: they felt empowered and grateful.

This experience helped them realise they had so much more than they initially thought. They recognised that they were blessed in many ways, prompting them to focus on what they had rather than dwelling on what they lacked.

Acts of kindness serve a true purpose; they empower you, fill you with gratitude and make you feel that 'life's not THAT bad'.

They give you the strength to be resilient.

Questions to Answer

- What is one thing that always makes you feel strong and capable?

  _____

- Write about a time when you faced a challenge and came out stronger on the other side.

  _____

- List three things you are grateful for today, no matter how small.
  _____

- Describe a situation where you felt overwhelmed. How did you cope with it?
  _____

- Write down a quote or mantra that inspires you to keep going when times get tough.
  _____

- Reflect on a recent mistake or failure. What did you learn from it?
  _____

- Write about someone you admire for their resilience. What qualities do they possess?
  _____

- Describe a time when you received support from a friend or loved one. How did it help you?
  _____

- List three things you can do today to take care of yourself and recharge.
  _____

Inspiring Quotes

It is really wonderful how much resilience there is in human nature. Let any obstructing cause, no matter what, be removed in any way, even by death, and we fly back to first principles of hope and enjoyment.

- Bram Stoker

The human capacity for burden is like bamboo – far more flexible than you'd ever believe at first glance.

- Jodi Picoult

I can't change the direction of the wind, but I can adjust my sails to always reach my destination.

- Jimmy Dean

Rock bottom became the solid foundation on which I rebuilt my life.

- J.K. Rowling

In the depth of winter, I finally learned that within me there lay an invincible summer.

- Albert Camus

10

Power of Self-Belief

YOU WILL NOT BELIEVE how challenging it has been for researchers to define self-belief. Some argue that it simply means believing in your ability to accomplish tasks, while others consider it synonymous with confidence. In reality, it encompasses both notions. It is that inner feeling that is consistently motivating you, saying, 'So what? You can do it!'

Self-belief acts as your personal cheerleader. When you face challenges or doubts, this supportive voice encourages you to persevere. It tells you, 'You have got this! Do not give up', helping you maintain a positive outlook even when situations become difficult.

Of all the superpowers you possess, self-belief is the strongest. It helps to shoo almost all types of noises that hinder your progress.

When you face a challenge, your brain sends signals through pathways — think of these pathways as roads in your brain. Self-belief activates the routes associated with motivation and positive feelings, releasing chemicals like dopamine that make you feel happy.

We have already learned that when we succeed, even in small tasks, our brain takes notice. This recognition not only makes us more aware of successes in the world around us but also strengthens the connection between believing in yourself and feeling positive. It creates a loop: you believe you can succeed, you take action, you achieve your goal and then your belief in yourself grows even stronger.

Power of Self-Belief

Self-belief is connected to everything we have discussed in this book so far – shooing off noises, healing emotional wounds, rewiring the brain and developing a resilient mind.

Self-belief is a skill, not an ability, that needs to be developed within you.

There is a difference between skill and ability. Ability refers to natural talents you are born with, while skill is something you learn through practice and experience.

Having strong self-belief can boost your self-esteem, which can help you develop strong self-confidence, self-respect, self-worth and self-acceptance.

While self-belief involves having confidence in your abilities, worth and potential to achieve your goals, self-esteem, on the other hand, is your overall evaluation of your worth as a person.

My ability to write and express myself, as well as to understand deeper meanings, was a natural gift. However, my self-belief wavered when my English teacher rejected my short story in school. This rejection led me to believe that I could not write good stories or articles, which lowered my self-esteem and made me stop participating in story-writing competitions. Why? Because that teacher said I was not good enough.

Self-belief can be shaken by even the smallest criticism. The person offering the critique often does not realise how deeply it can affect someone, especially at a young age when you may not even fully understand what all of this is about.

I feel grateful that I had my parents to help me develop my self-belief and instil its importance in my life.

Building self-belief to develop strong self-esteem is not always easy. It takes courage to confront moments of doubt and fear, to face them boldly and say, 'Not today.' It takes kindness, too, to treat ourselves with compassion, embracing our flaws and imperfections as part of what makes us beautifully human.

Imagine you are about to take on a big challenge, like climbing a mountain or acing a test. What thoughts come to mind? This is where mindset plays a crucial role as a powerful tool for building self-belief.

Mindset is like the lens through which we see the world and ourselves.

There are two main types of mindsets: a fixed mindset and a growth mindset.

A fixed mindset is the belief that our abilities and intelligence are set in stone. We think, 'I am either good at something or I am not, and there is nothing I can do about it.' In contrast, a growth mindset is the belief that we can improve and grow through effort and practice.

With a growth mindset, we think, 'I may not be great at this now, but with practice and perseverance, I can get better.'

Research has shown that our mindset can have a significant impact on our success and happiness.

Studies by psychologist Carol Dweck indicate that students with a growth mindset are more likely to embrace challenges, persist in the face of setbacks and achieve higher levels of success compared with those who have a fixed mindset.

Even Barack Obama, the former president of the United States, said in his book *Dreams from My Father: A Story of Race and Inheritance*, 'The best way to not feel hopeless is to get up and do something. Do not wait for good things to happen to you. If you go out and make some good things happen, you will fill the world with hope, you will fill yourself with hope.'

So how does the power of mindset relate to building self-belief?

Consider it this way: if you believe that your abilities can improve with effort and practice, you are more likely to take on challenges and persevere, even when faced with difficulties. This kind of resilience and determination is at the heart of self-belief.

You can build the self-belief you need to tackle any challenge and shoo all the noises that come your way by adopting a growth mindset.

Have you heard or read about Helen Keller?

Maybe not.

Helen Keller was an American author, political activist and lecturer who wrote several books and delivered numerous speeches. What if I told you she was blind and deaf? Hard to believe, right? However, this is a fact.

What allowed her to overcome these limitations was her growth mindset. It is important to understand that how and where you are born will not decide how and where you will die. Helen realised she had to do something big in life.

Instead of feeling sorry for herself, giving up or blaming her circumstances, she believed in her ability to learn and achieve great things.

With the help of her teacher, Anne Sullivan, Helen learned to communicate using sign language and even how to read braille.

Helen did not stop there. She went on to graduate from college, become an author and advocate for the rights of people with disabilities.

Despite her disabilities, Helen travelled the world and inspired millions of people with her courage and determination.

People told her it was impossible. They said it was crazy and that she needed to stop or she would ruin her life.

But Helen was determined. Her self-belief remained strong, and her growth mindset propelled her forward.

Her story reminds us that no matter what noises we hear, we can achieve our dreams if we believe in ourselves, work hard and shoo these noises.

Helen Keller once said, 'Keep your face to the sunshine and you cannot see a shadow.'

What she meant by this quote is that we need to maintain a positive attitude. When we focus on the good things in life, we are less likely to notice the negative aspects as much. It is about focusing on the bright side and not letting negative things pull us down.

We should always look up, for those who focus downwards miss the beauty of the sky – where the sun rises, the stars twinkle and the moon shines.

Seven Steps to Cultivate Strong Self-belief

- Choose progress over perfection.
- Track your growth, even if it is by 1 per cent, and note it somewhere.
- Stop comparing yourself with others. Know that only you are your competition.
- Practise positive self-talk.
- Take your failure as a stepping stone, learn from it and improvise.
- Practise assertiveness.
- Keep reminding yourself of your 'why'.

Affirmations for Self-Belief

- I believe in myself and my abilities.
- I live with success and happiness.
- I trust myself to handle whatever comes my way.
- I am capable, strong and resilient.
- I deserve all the good things life has to offer.
- I am confident in my decisions and actions.
- I am enough just as I am.
- I am loved and respected.
- I embrace challenges as opportunities to grow.
- I am the architect of my own destiny.

11

Build a Supportive Network

IMAGINE SAILING ACROSS THE vast ocean of life, navigating its unpredictable waves and winds. As you continue your journey, you understand that regardless of how skilled a sailor you are, having a supportive network is like having a sturdy anchor that keeps you grounded amid life's storms.

Before discussing the importance of building a supportive network, let us first address why being a leader in your own life is crucial.

Being a leader does not necessarily mean being at the forefront of every situation. Instead, it involves taking charge of your destiny, making decisions that align with your values and guiding yourself towards your goals. As renowned leadership expert John C. Maxwell once said, 'A leader is one who knows the way, goes the way and shows the way.'

Being a leader in your own life gives you power. It is like having the remote control for your journey – you get to decide which channels to tune into and where you want to go. You are not just aimlessly drifting but intentionally steering your ship with purpose.

Confidence is another key aspect of being a leader. When you take the lead, you believe in yourself and your abilities. You carry a certain swagger, an inner assurance that you can handle whatever challenges life throws your way. It is like wearing a superhero cape beneath your everyday clothes.

Additionally, being a leader means being resilient. You know how to bounce back when things do not go your way. Instead of crumbling under pressure, you stand tall and face challenges head-on. It is like having a superpower that transforms setbacks into stepping stones for success.

Most importantly, being a leader does not mean going it alone. In fact, it is quite the opposite. As a leader, you attract a team of supporters, cheerleaders and confidants. They are your ride-or-die squad, your backup dancers in the dance of life.

This is where building a supportive network comes in.

Being a leader is not just about calling the shots; it is about surrounding yourself with people who uplift you and have your back no matter what. They serve as your sounding board, your voice of reason, your partners in crime.

As Oprah Winfrey, media mogul and philanthropist, famously said, 'Surround yourself with only people who are going to lift you higher.'

A supportive network not only celebrates our victories but also provides comfort during our struggles. When you have a strong supportive network, you do not feel isolated when facing failure.

Think of your favourite actor, such as Salman Khan. As a devoted fan, you admire him immensely. Imagine he is releasing hit after hit, but suddenly his movies start to flop. What would you do?

A loyal fan would continue to support him. So what if one movie failed? We still love you. We will wait for the next one.

This is what having a supportive network means.

While a supportive network is essential, it is equally important not to become over-dependent on it.

Relying solely on others for validation, direction or solutions can lead to a sense of disempowerment and diminish one's ability to navigate life's challenges independently.

As the philosopher Ralph Waldo Emerson once remarked, 'Self-trust is the first secret of success.' Building self-trust and resilience allows us to draw strength from within and seek support from our network as a supplement rather than a crutch.

Steve Jobs, co-founder of Apple, once said, 'Great things in business are never done by one person; they are done by a team of people', and I could not agree more.

I know I have loyal readers who will buy my new book without considering the genre or whether it interests them. They trust me, my words and my vision, and I am truly grateful for the supportive network I have built over the years.

Build a Supportive Network

But how did I achieve this?

Here are some practical steps for building a strong, supportive network:

- Identify the type of support you need, whether it is career advice, emotional support or personal encouragement.
- Start by reaching out to friends, family, colleagues and acquaintances whom you trust and feel comfortable with.
- Look for clubs, organisations or online groups that align with your interests or professional goals. These can be great places to meet like-minded individuals.
- Attend networking events, workshops, seminars or conferences in your industry or community. Be open to starting conversations and making new connections.
- Volunteer for causes or organisations that are meaningful to you. This is a great way to meet people with similar values and passions.
- Use social media platforms like LinkedIn, X (formerly Twitter) or Facebook to connect with professionals, experts and peers in your field.
- When building relationships, be genuine, authentic and supportive of others. Show interest in their lives and be willing to offer help and support in return.
- After meeting someone new, follow up with them via email, phone calls or social media. Stay connected by checking in periodically and nurturing the relationship over time.
- Participate in workshops, training programmes or professional development courses. These settings provide opportunities to meet and connect with others who share your interests or career aspirations.
- Do not be afraid to ask friends, family or colleagues to introduce you to people in their networks who may be able to offer support or guidance.

12

Boundaries to Protect Yourself

Alright, let us discuss the concept of boundaries. Think of them as fences around a house. They are not just meant to keep people out; they are also essential for keeping what is inside safe and comfortable. Boundaries serve a similar purpose for our emotions and mental well-being.

So what exactly are boundaries?

They are like lines drawn in the sand – those invisible markers that say, 'This is me, this is my space and these are my feelings.' Boundaries help us define who we are and what we are comfortable with.

But boundaries are not only about keeping certain people at arm's length; they are also about welcoming the right people into your life.

Let me give you an example.

Imagine a friend who constantly unloads their drama on you, expecting you to act as their therapist 24/7. While it is important to support your friends and help them, you need to establish boundaries when their behaviour starts to impact your own mental health.

When you are on an aeroplane, they always tell you to put on your own oxygen mask before helping others, right? I think it is a similar principle when it comes to mental health.

You need to be assertive enough to take a stand for yourself and remind yourself, 'I need to take care of myself first before I can be there for you or anyone else.'

It is essential to set boundaries and say no when necessary.

This is not just about refusing others; it is also about saying yes to yourself. Recognise your limits and honour them. For instance, if you need alone time to recharge, you might set aside an evening each week for some much-needed 'me time'. Alternatively, if you are in a relationship where your partner tends to cross your emotional boundaries, it is important to have a conversation and establish ground rules for how you want to be treated.

But boundaries are not just about protecting ourselves from others; they are also about protecting ourselves from our own behaviour.

It might sound a bit strange, but consider this: how many times have you allowed negative self-talk or unrealistic expectations to spiral out of control, leaving you feeling stressed and burnt out? This is where boundaries play a crucial role. They serve as a shield against our inner demons, reminding us to be kind to ourselves and cut ourselves some slack.

So why are boundaries so essential for our mental health and for protecting ourselves? It is because when we do not have clear boundaries, it is easy for others to take advantage of us, which can leave us feeling drained and resentful. However, when we establish boundaries – when we know what we will and will not tolerate – we are taking back control of our lives. We are essentially saying, 'This is who I am, this is what I stand for and I am not letting anyone undermine that.'

In summary, boundaries are like fences around our hearts and minds. They help keep the positive influences in and the negative ones out. Once you start setting and enforcing your boundaries, you will likely feel like a new person – stronger, happier and more in control of your own destiny.

You might be curious about how boundaries relate to our topic of shooing the noises from our lives.

Boundaries play a crucial role in shooing the noises because they help us create a sense of clarity and focus amid life's chaos. Just like turning down the volume on a loud TV, setting boundaries allows us to filter out distractions and prioritise what truly matters to us.

By establishing these boundaries, we can minimise the noise – unnecessary chatter, overwhelming demands and toxic relationships – that can drown out our inner voice, leaving us overwhelmed and drained. Instead, we create a quieter, more peaceful environment where we can attune ourselves, listen to our needs and focus on what brings us joy and fulfilment.

In essence, boundaries help us shoo the noises by allowing us to create a space where we can thrive – mentally, emotionally and spiritually. Boundaries empower us to take control of our lives, protect our well-being and cultivate a sense of balance and harmony amid the hustle and bustle of everyday life.

Now that we understand what boundaries are and why it is important to set them, let us look at the different types of boundaries.

First, we have physical boundaries. These relate to personal space, like the invisible bubble around us that we prefer others not to invade. For example, imagine you are sitting in a crowded bus and someone is practically breathing down your neck. That is not cool. Your physical boundary is signalling, 'Hey, back off a bit – I need some breathing room!'

Physical boundaries play a crucial role in many situations, particularly personal interactions. For instance, if someone touches you without permission – like giving you a hug you are not comfortable with or a pat on the back that feels a bit too unfamiliar – it can be quite unsettling. In those moments, you might think, 'Excuse me, can you not?' This is a reminder that we have the right to control our personal space.

Essentially, physical boundaries revolve around respecting our personal space and physical comfort levels. It is like drawing a line in the sand and saying, 'This is my bubble, and I decide who gets to enter.' When someone crosses that line, it is normal to feel uneasy or uncomfortable. After all, it is our space, and we have every right to protect it.

Then come emotional boundaries – they are like a shield that protects our feelings and thoughts. Imagine you are confiding in a friend about something personal, like a dream you are pursuing or a fear you are facing. When you open up and show your vulnerability –

only to be met with harsh criticism or judgement – it can be hurtful. That is when your emotional boundary comes into play.

It acts like an inner guard saying, 'Wait a minute, that is not acceptable.' It is crucial to acknowledge that your feelings are valid and deserve respect. We each have the right to our own thoughts, feelings and experiences, and no one should have the power to belittle or shame us for them.

Emotional boundaries are about establishing limits on how others treat us and how we allow ourselves to be treated. It is important to surround ourselves with people who uplift and support us rather than those who bring us down. When someone crosses that line and tries to dim our light, it is essential to speak up and say, 'Hey, that is not okay with me.' Ultimately, our emotional well-being is worth protecting, no matter what.

Another type of boundary you need to set is a time boundary!

Time boundaries act like a superhero cape that helps us manage our schedules and maintain our sanity. You know that feeling when you have a gazillion things on your to-do list and not enough hours in the day? It is like being caught in a whirlwind of busyness, leaving you feeling totally overwhelmed.

Fortunately, time boundaries are here to save us from that chaos. They involve setting limits on how much we commit to and ensuring we do not spread ourselves too thin. It is essentially saying, 'Hold on, I cannot do everything, and that is perfectly okay.'

If you are feeling overwhelmed with work, social events, family obligations and everything in between, it might be time to establish some time boundaries. Instead of trying to do everything and ending up exhausted, consider saying no to that extra project at work or reducing your social commitments to create some breathing room for yourself.

It is also important to prioritise what truly matters. Take the time to figure out your top priorities – whether it is spending quality time with loved ones, pursuing your passions or simply taking a moment to relax – and make sure to carve out time for those activities.

One common misconception about setting time boundaries is that it is selfish or lazy. In reality, it is about taking care of ourselves and prioritising what truly matters. When we establish time boundaries, it is not because we do not want to help others or be there for them; rather, we recognise that our time and energy are precious resources that need to be used wisely.

Sometimes, people may perceive setting time boundaries as being rude or uncaring, especially when it involves saying no to invitations or requests for assistance. This fear of being judged often leads us to compromise our time boundaries.

But the truth is, setting boundaries is actually an important act of self-respect and self-care. It involves recognising our own limits and honouring our needs, even if it occasionally disappoints others.

Another common misconception is that setting time boundaries indicates a lack of ambition or hard work. In reality, it is quite the opposite. By setting boundaries around our time and commitments, we position ourselves for success. This practice provides us with the space and freedom to focus on our goals, pursue our passions and perform at our best.

Let us not forget the misconception that setting boundaries means closing ourselves off from others or being antisocial. That could not be further from the truth. In fact, setting time boundaries can actually strengthen our relationships and deepen our connections with others. By being honest and upfront about our availability and priorities, we foster open communication and mutual respect in our interactions.

So the next time someone misunderstands your time boundaries, remember that it is not about being selfish, lazy or uncaring. It is about taking care of yourself, respecting your limits and creating the space you need to thrive. And that is something worth standing up for, regardless of what others may think.

Trust me, you will thank yourself later when you feel more balanced, focused and ready to tackle whatever life throws your way. Setting time boundaries is essential for achieving this.

Now, let us talk about relational boundaries.

Having relational boundaries is like drawing a line in the sand to define how we want to be treated in our relationships. Often, we do not even realise when a relationship has turned toxic.

A toxic relationship is like a dark cloud overshadowing your sunny day. It can occur in any relationship – whether with a friend, partner or even a relative – that leaves you feeling drained, unhappy or downright miserable.

Now, toxic relationships can take many forms. They might involve a friend who constantly puts you down, makes you feel small or spreads gossip about you. It could be a partner who is controlling, manipulative or downright abusive. Even family members can sometimes be toxic; for instance, a parent who is overly critical or a sibling who constantly belittles you.

The reality is that toxic relationships are like poison; they gradually erode your self-esteem, happiness and sense of worth. The longer you remain in these relationships, the harder it can be to break free and reclaim your life.

But here is the good news. You do not have to remain trapped in a toxic relationship forever. You can set boundaries, stand up for yourself and surround yourself with people who lift you rather than bring you down.

Setting boundaries with toxic relatives can be especially tricky. After all, they are family, right? However, it is important to remember that sharing your DNA does not grant anyone a free pass to treat you poorly. You have every right to distance yourself from toxic relatives, whether that means limiting your interactions with them or cutting ties altogether.

I understand that walking away from family can be incredibly difficult, but sometimes prioritising your well-being is the healthiest choice you can make.

It is essential to surround yourself with people who love and support you unconditionally. Do not hesitate to seek help if you need it.

Remember, you deserve to be treated with kindness, respect and love – no matter who you are or where you come from. Do not let toxic relationships hold you back. Take control of your life, set clear boundaries and surround yourself with the positivity and support you deserve.

The thing that requires the most courage is saying no. It is often easier to say yes to avoid conflict, please others or maintain a relationship, even when it goes against our needs or boundaries. But summoning the courage to say no is an act of self-respect and self-care.

When we say no, we are asserting our boundaries and prioritising our well-being. It takes courage to stand firm in our convictions and to prioritise ourselves, even if it might disappoint or inconvenience others. Saying no means being honest with ourselves and others about what we can and cannot handle, which requires courage.

Moreover, saying no can be particularly challenging when we fear rejection or judgement from others. It takes courage to confront these fears and assert ourselves in the face of potential disapproval or disappointment. But ultimately, saying no empowers us to live authentically and honour our needs and values.

First, it is crucial to recognise that saying no is not a selfish act; rather, it is an act of self-preservation. Just like putting on your own oxygen mask before assisting others on a plane, prioritising your own needs and well-being is essential for your overall health and happiness.

So why is saying no important? For starters, it helps prevent burnout.

When we constantly say yes to every request or obligation that comes our way, we risk spreading ourselves too thin, depleting our energy reserves. Saying no allows us to conserve our energy and focus on what truly matters to us.

Additionally, saying no helps us establish and maintain boundaries in our relationships. It communicates to others that our time, energy and resources are valuable and finite, and that we are not willing to compromise our well-being just to please everyone else.

However, let us be honest – saying no often makes us feel guilty. So how can we say no without feeling that guilt?

- **Be honest and direct**: Instead of making excuses or beating around the bush, be honest about your reasons for saying no. You do not owe anyone a lengthy explanation, but a simple 'I am sorry, but I cannot commit to that right now' can suffice.
- **Practise self-compassion**: Remind yourself that it is okay to prioritise your own needs and well-being. You are not obligated to say yes to everything, and you deserve to take care of yourself without feeling guilty.
- **Offer alternatives**: If you are unable to fulfil a request, offer alternative solutions or compromises when possible. This shows your willingness to help, even if it differs from the original request.
- **Practise assertiveness**: Assertiveness is about standing up for yourself and your needs in a way that is neither aggressive nor passive. To express your boundaries confidently, practise assertive communication techniques, such as using 'I' statements and maintaining eye contact.

Remember, saying no is not a rejection of others; rather, it is a way to prioritise your own needs, and you should not feel guilty about it. By learning to say no when necessary and setting boundaries, you are taking an important step towards preserving your well-being and achieving a more balanced and fulfilling life.

Another challenging factor is setting boundaries in a professional context, particularly at work.

One of the biggest reasons people struggle with setting boundaries at work is the fear of conflict. They worry about upsetting colleagues or supervisors by saying 'no' or expressing their needs. However, it is important to remember that healthy conflict can lead to positive outcomes and stronger relationships. The key is to approach these conversations with respect and empathy. Workplace cultures can vary significantly. For instance, I am a freelancer working with various clients across different industries, while you might be employed at a multinational corporation or a startup. In some environments, there may be a perception that saying 'no' or setting boundaries is a sign of weakness or a lack of dedication. This fear can lead to concerns that your 'boss' might give you poor performance reviews, hindering your chances of promotion or even resulting in job loss.

However, it is essential to acknowledge that everyone has limits, and prioritising self-care does not make you any less committed to your job. In smaller companies or startups, employees often find themselves wearing multiple hats and taking on tasks outside their job descriptions. While being adaptable is valuable, it is crucial to clarify expectations and boundaries to avoid burnout and resentment.

In certain industries or companies, there is a prevalent culture of overwork, where long hours and constant availability are glorified. Many of my clients choose their mental well-being over such toxic work environments and decide to switch jobs. That is a strong example of setting boundaries in the workplace. However, I understand that not everyone has the option to simply leave a job when the working hours and environment are unsatisfactory. Many people feel guilty about setting boundaries, fearing they will disappoint their team or miss opportunities.

So how do you set these boundaries?

It is all about communication and knowing your limits. With colleagues, it is perfectly acceptable to politely decline additional tasks if you are already busy. You might say, 'I would love to help, but I have a lot on my plate right now. Can we revisit this next week?' This approach sets a clear boundary without damaging your working relationship.

When dealing with supervisors, it is crucial to establish realistic expectations from the beginning. If you are consistently asked to work late or take on more than you can handle, it is time for an open conversation about your workload and boundaries. Remember, it is not just about saying 'no' – it is about working together to find compromises and solutions that benefit both parties.

And let us not forget about clients. Although technically external to your workplace, they can still encroach on your time and energy if you let them. Be firm yet polite in setting boundaries around response times, availability and the scope of work. For example, you might set specific office hours for client communication or establish a clear timeline for project deliverables.

Setting boundaries is not selfish or standoffish; it is about taking care of yourself so that you can perform at your best in the workplace. Remember:

- **Communicate clearly**: Be transparent about your needs, limitations and priorities. Use assertive yet respectful language when expressing your boundaries to colleagues and supervisors.
- **Lead by example**: By modelling healthy boundaries and work-life balance, you can inspire others to do the same. Share your experiences and strategies for managing workload and stress in a sustainable way.
- **Seek support**: If you are struggling to set boundaries or facing resistance, do not hesitate to seek support from HR, a mentor or a trusted colleague. They can offer guidance and perspective to help you navigate challenging situations.

There is a thin line between stepping out of your comfort zone and setting boundaries. Both sound contradictory, right? But both are equally important for us to shoo the majority of noises in our lives.

Stepping out of your comfort zone while setting boundaries is like trying to find the perfect balance between adventure and protection. Trust me, it is worth figuring out.

So let us break it down.

Stepping out of your comfort zone is about shaking things up, trying new experiences and expanding your horizons. It is like deciding to take a salsa class even though you have two left feet or volunteering for a project at work that is far outside your usual routine. It might feel a bit scary initially, but this is how we grow and discover our hidden talents and strengths.

On the other hand, setting boundaries is like creating your own bubble – a safe space where you feel comfortable, respected and in control. It involves saying 'yes' to the things that energise you and 'no' to what drains your energy or makes you feel uneasy. This could mean telling your friends you need some alone time or setting clear workload expectations with your boss. Boundaries serve as a protective barrier, safeguarding your mental and emotional well-being from unwanted stressors.

But here is the thing – finding the right balance between these two is not always easy. Sometimes, we become so focused on seeking new experiences that we forget to set boundaries, especially when things feel overwhelming. Other times, we are so focused on protecting our space that we miss out on opportunities for growth and adventure.

So how do we achieve that perfect balance?

It all comes down to tuning in to our inner compass – the little voice inside that knows what is best for our well-being. Pay attention to your feelings in different situations. Are you feeling excited and energised or are you starting to feel stressed and drained? Recognise those signals and do not hesitate to speak up and set boundaries when necessary.

But also, do not be afraid to take risks and try new things. Stepping out of your comfort zone can be intimidating, but that is where the real magic happens. Whether it is finally starting that passion project you have been dreaming about or signing up for that solo trip you have always wanted to take. Embrace the unknown and trust that you can handle whatever comes your way.

It is also okay if you stumble along the way. Finding balance is a journey, and experiencing ups and downs is normal. Just keep listening to your inner compass, honouring your boundaries and embracing the adventure of life.

So whether it is giving ourselves space to breathe, protecting our emotional well-being, managing our time effectively or nurturing positive relationships, boundaries are the secret sauce that keeps everything running smoothly. Although it may take some practice to get comfortable with them, once you start, you will feel like a whole new person – stronger, happier and ready to take on the world.

Inspiring Quotes

You have to set boundaries in every relationship. Without boundaries, you expose yourself to being taken advantage of.
- Oprah Winfrey

Your personal boundaries protect the inner core of your identity and your right to choices.
- Gerard Manley Hopkins

Boundaries are fences that protect your time, energy and well-being.
- Elizabeth Gilbert

Setting boundaries is a way of caring for myself. It does not make me mean, selfish or uncaring because I don't do things your way. I care about me too.
- Christine Morgan

13

Mindfulness

IMAGINE YOU ARE EATING an apple. Mindfulness means truly focusing on the taste, texture and even the sound of the crunch when you take a bite.

Mindfulness is simply about being aware of your surroundings and your inner self. Mindfulness de-noises your energy system and lets you hear only what you want to hear.

It is about giving your full attention to whatever you are doing, whether walking, talking or just breathing.

Now, why does this matter? Life can get incredibly busy and sometimes overwhelming, right?

Mindfulness helps us slow down and take a breather. It is like hitting the pause button in the middle of chaos.

When we are mindful, we are less likely to get lost in worries about the past or the future. Instead, we focus on the present moment, fully experiencing it. Mindfulness builds resilience, strengthening us to shoo away the noises and stay committed to our goals and dreams. Practising mindfulness can actually help us deal with tough situations, like stress or anxiety, which are some of the major noises in our lives.

The best part? Anyone can practise mindfulness! You do not need fancy equipment or special skills – just a willingness to try it.

People often confuse mindfulness with meditation. While meditation is one of the ways to practise mindfulness, there are both formal and informal methods of mindfulness practice. Formal mindfulness includes activities like meditation and yoga, whereas informal mindfulness practice can be as simple as walking in the garden or watching the rain fall.

Mindfulness is not a new concept; it dates back thousands of years. Buddhism has made mindfulness a core element of its teachings.

In ancient times, people in regions like India and China began incorporating mindfulness into their spiritual and meditation practices.

Approximately 2,500 years ago in India, Siddhartha Gautama, who later became The Buddha, significantly contributed to the spread of mindfulness. He taught his followers to be fully present at the moment and to pay attention to their thoughts, feelings and sensations without judgement. This practice helped them find peace and happiness in their lives.

Around the same time in China, Taoist and Confucian teachings also emphasised mindfulness as a way to live in harmony with nature and the world around them.

In the 20th century, mindfulness began to gain attention in the West, largely due to people like Jon Kabat-Zinn. He developed a programme called Mindfulness-Based Stress Reduction (MBSR) to help people cope with pain, illness and stress.

Since then, mindfulness has become extremely popular around the world.

Scientists have studied its benefits, schools have started incorporating it into their curricula for children, and millions of people practise it every day to find calmness and clarity in their busy lives.

Many successful and notable people engage in mindfulness practices every day to shoo away the noises and focus on what is important to them.

Jeff Weiner, the former CEO of LinkedIn, has openly discussed his mindfulness practices and their positive impact on his leadership style and overall well-being. In an interview with CNBC, Weiner emphasised the importance of mindfulness in managing stress and making better decisions. He noted that mindfulness helps him stay focused, prioritise effectively and maintain a sense of balance amid the demands of his role as a CEO.

Weiner also talked about integrating mindfulness into LinkedIn's company culture. Under his leadership, LinkedIn offered mindfulness and meditation programmes for employees, recognising the benefits of these practices in enhancing employee engagement and productivity.

Another notable example is Ray Dalio, the founder of Bridgewater Associates, one of the world's largest hedge funds. Dalio has openly shared his mindfulness and meditation practices in interviews, articles and his book *Principles: Life and Work*. In his book, Dalio discusses the importance of mindfulness, meditation and reflection in decision-making and personal growth.

Additionally, the 'Silent Hour' concept by Napoleon Hill, which we discussed earlier in this book, focuses on practising mindfulness for one hour every day.

Scientists, particularly in the fields of neuroscience and psychology, have been studying how mindfulness impacts our brains. They have found that mindfulness can strengthen and activate certain areas of the brain, especially those responsible for attention and emotional regulation. Mindfulness helps us handle tough emotions and think more clearly.

In fact, counsellors and doctors often recommend incorporating mindfulness into daily routines, especially for patients dealing with stress, depression and anxiety-related problems.

Moreover, mindfulness benefits not just our mental health but also our physical well-being. It is a proven fact that practising mindfulness can lead to overall better health by lowering blood pressure and boosting the immune system.

People who practise mindfulness often experience greater happiness, relaxation, focus and success.

But is this relevant to the topic we are discussing in this book?

As I mentioned earlier, everything is interconnected.

Your brain possesses abilities that you may not even imagine. Just like our fingerprints, each brain is unique. This is why it is said that we all are special in our own ways.

Mindfulness is one of the most powerful tools for quieting the noises, both internal and external. It helps us connect with our authentic selves. The various noises discussed earlier in this book can be blocked by embracing mindfulness – it is *that* effective.

Here are seven small steps to practising mindful living every day:

- When you wake up in the morning, do not check your phone.
- Whatever your first drink of the morning is, savour every sip.
- Spend some time with your houseplants. Try doing this in the morning.
- When you experience any low-vibrational feelings like sadness, anger, guilt, resentment or anxiety, stop, take a pause and drink water before you react.
- Make your bed.
- Take a walk intuitively, without planning or thinking about where or why.
- Look at your vision board or vision journal for at least five minutes every day.

Get a Clear Vision

Though there are many ways to gain a clear vision of what you want in life, I want to discuss one method that has helped me and millions of people around the world. This tried-and-tested approach can enhance your mindfulness, rewire your brain and support your personal growth, enabling you to manifest your dreams and desires.

This method is known as the vision board technique.

A vision board is a visual representation of your goals, dreams and desires. It resembles a collage made up of images, words and symbols that inspire and motivate you. By creating a vision board, you can bring your aspirations to life and keep them in sight as you work towards achieving them.

Mindfulness

Mindfulness involves being fully present in the moment and paying attention to your thoughts, feelings and surroundings without judgement. Creating a vision board is a mindful practice because it allows you to focus intentionally on your goals and aspirations. This process helps you connect with your deepest desires and fosters a sense of clarity and purpose in your life.

Moreover, creating a vision board can be a form of self-discovery and personal growth. It encourages you to reflect on what truly matters to you and visualise the life you wish to create. By engaging in this creative practice, you actively shape your future and take steps towards manifesting your dreams.

Overall, a vision board is a simple yet powerful tool.

So how can you create your own vision board?

First things first, you do not necessarily need a 'board' for your vision board. You can use chart paper or even a diary to create one. Personally, I create my vision board on the first few pages of my yearly journal. This way, I see my vision board every day, and it remains personal to me. This approach works well if you live in a joint family like I do. Otherwise, feel free to create a giant vision board if that is what you prefer!

Now, gather some magazines, newspapers, photos, flyers or any material that contains images. Look for pictures that resonate with your life goals. For instance, if you find a picture of a house in a magazine and you aspire to own a similar one, cut out that image and place it on your vision board. You can also include images representing other goals you wish to manifest, such as a specific card, a desired amount of money, a meaningful relationship, your dream job, a successful business, admission to a college, travel to a particular destination or even a golden YouTube Play Button. In addition to images, feel free to include handwritten notes, affirmations and quotes that reflect and resonate with your goals, dreams and desires.

Once you have created your vision board, spend a few minutes each day looking at it, touching it with your fingers and visualising your goals.

Your vision board serves as a powerful reminder of what you want to achieve in your life. Use it as a source of inspiration and motivation to take meaningful action towards your objectives. Break your goals down into manageable steps and consistently work towards bringing your vision to life.

5-4-3-2-1 Method

If you are unsure how to start practising mindful living, consider trying the 5-4-3-2-1 method. This approach is excellent for beginners and helps you become more aware of your surroundings.

The 5-4-3-2-1 method is a simple mindfulness exercise designed to help ground you in the present moment and alleviate feelings of stress or anxiety. It involves engaging your senses to increase awareness of your immediate experiences.

Here is how it works.

To begin, whether you are using a diary, journal, paper or notes on your phone, follow these steps:

- Find a comfortable position to sit or stand. You may choose to close your eyes if it feels right for you, but it is not necessary.
- Begin by taking a slow, deep breath through your nose, then exhale slowly through your mouth. Allow yourself to relax and release any tension you may be holding in your body.
- Now, focus on your immediate environment and engage your senses.

5 – Write five things you see
4 – Write four things you feel
3 – Write three things you hear
2 – Write two things you smell
1 – Write one thing you can taste

This exercise has no specific rules, so you can practise it at home, in the office or even on the metro during your commute.

- Write down anything that comes to mind. It is similar to playing a rapid-fire game with yourself but it is more relaxed and slower-paced.
- During the exercise, focus on staying present and fully immersing yourself in each sensory experience. If your mind begins to wander or distracting thoughts arise, gently redirect your attention back to your senses and the present moment.
- Once you finish, take a moment to express gratitude for the ability to experience the richness of your surroundings and the present moment.

The 5-4-3-2-1 method is a quick and effective way to shift your attention away from anxious or distracting thoughts and anchor yourself in the present. It can be practised anywhere and at any time, making it a valuable tool for cultivating mindfulness and reducing stress in daily life.

Your Pause Button

Life can be noisy and finding a mute button to shoo away the noises is essential. While muting and shooing the noises requires the techniques discussed in this book, there is a simple method – your pause button – that can quickly shift your focus from the negative to the positive within seconds and enhance your mindfulness.

To implement this, choose something that triggers you or serves as a reminder to 'pause' for a second. This 'something' can be anything that you can see or hear, like a car horn, a siren, an image on the computer, a fridge magnet, a photograph, a ringtone, a bird or anything else that resonates with you.

Whenever you see or hear this special 'something', take a moment to pause. Notice your surroundings, reflect on what is happening or simply express gratitude by saying thank you, invoking God's name, reciting a mantra or stating an affirmation.

For instance, my grandfather had a habit of saying 'Hari Om' whenever he burped. I am sure someone in your family has a similar habit of saying something when they yawn or burp. These expressions serve as a common form of a pause button.

As for me, I have the habit of saying 'Namaste' and 'Thank you' whenever I see a photo or idol of my God or pass by a temple. I also express gratitude or make a wish when I see 11:11. These are my personal pause buttons.

So tonight, when you sleep, just think about what your pause button can be and assign a word, mantra or affirmation to it if you do not want to do all the thinking and breathing exercises.

Pamper Yourself

Pampering is one of the most underrated acts of mindfulness.

Girls may notice that the world seems to pause for them when they apply nail paint; their entire focus is on that one activity. Similarly, boys experience this mindfulness when they shave their beards. During these moments, they are completely aware of every stroke they make and every subtle texture it creates. They can even notice the slightest imperfections. This is the essence of practising mindfulness.

Pampering provides a nurturing and rejuvenating experience that allows us to reconnect with our inner selves and cultivate a sense of well-being.

In today's fast-paced world, where demands and distractions abound, taking time for self-care is essential for maintaining balance and harmony in life. By pampering ourselves, we connect with the present moment, quiet our busy minds and honour our bodies and spirits with loving attention.

One of the fundamental aspects of mindfulness is being fully present in the moment, without judgement or distraction. Engaging in pampering activities, such as taking a soothing bath, enjoying a grooming session or receiving a relaxing massage, allows us the opportunity to immerse ourselves completely in the experience.

We savour the sensations, textures and aromas surrounding us, allowing ourselves to be fully present with each breath and every movement. This heightened awareness of the present moment fosters a deep sense of relaxation and inner peace, enabling us to let go of worries about the past or anxieties about the future.

Moreover, pampering oneself mindfully involves cultivating an attitude of self-compassion and kindness towards oneself.

Often, we can be our own harshest critics, constantly striving for perfection and pushing ourselves beyond our limits. However, through pampering activities, we can practise self-love and acceptance, embracing ourselves just as we are in the present moment.

By treating ourselves with gentleness and care, we acknowledge our inherent worth and reaffirm our right to prioritise our well-being and happiness. I strongly believe mindful pampering is a powerful antidote to stress and anxiety.

In today's hyper-connected world, where technology and screens dominate our attention, it is easy to become mentally and emotionally drained.

Pampering activities offer a respite from the demands of daily life, providing a sacred space for relaxation and rejuvenation. Whether it is indulging in a luxurious spa treatment, spending time in nature, lighting your favourite scented candle or simply enjoying a quiet moment of solitude, pampering allows us to recharge our batteries and replenish our energy. As a result, we feel refreshed and revitalised.

Incorporating mindfulness into these pampering activities can also enhance our overall sense of gratitude and joy.

When we approach pampering as a mindful practice, we become more attuned to the simple pleasures and blessings that surround us each day. Whether it is feeling the warmth of the sun on our skin, enjoying the fragrance of blooming flowers or listening to the laughter of loved ones, mindfulness invites us to savour these moments with a sense of wonder and appreciation.

So what can you do?

Spend at least ten minutes pampering yourself. This can be as easy as wearing your favourite outfit or treating yourself to your favourite chocolate.

Selective Minimalism

Have you ever noticed that Mark Zuckerberg, the founder of Meta (which includes Facebook, Instagram, WhatsApp and more), always seems to wear the same grey T-shirt? It has become somewhat of a trademark for him, has it not?

Interestingly, there is a meaningful concept behind this: minimalism.

Until my teenage years, I did not realise that this lifestyle had a specific term. My dad practised minimalism, and my brother, Swapnil, still embraces it to this day.

I remember when I was a kid, my dad used to declutter our house every three months. He would ask all of us to bring items that were broken or that we had not touched in the last three months (except for artefacts and decorative pieces). It became a family task, and everyone had to participate. My dad always said that if you have not 'used' an item in the last three months, you probably do not need it – you are just hoarding it. He encouraged us to pass it on to someone who actually needs it or discard it. He would say, 'A clutter-free home invites success and growth.'

Everyone in my house had a neat, organised cupboard filled only with things that were useful or meaningful to them. In contrast, I was the one who hoarded. My cupboard was cluttered and messy. Every two to three weeks, I would end up spending at least two hours cleaning because I could never find what I needed.

I often heard comments like, 'Asking you for something is pointless because it will take you an hour.' This made me feel bad, but it also made me realise that something was off about my lifestyle.

I, too, became frustrated when I could not locate items in my cupboard, even when I tried to keep it organised. This experience helped me to understand the importance of minimalism.

Over time, I realised that our schools also practise minimalism. As a kid, when I watched American TV shows like *Small Wonder*, *That's So Raven* and *High School Musical*, I thought their schools were so cool because they did not have uniforms. Meanwhile, in India, we were required to wear uniforms, which I thought was uncool. I complained about it throughout my school life. However, when I started college, I enjoyed dressing up in my favourite clothes for the first few months. Eventually, I felt it was a waste of time and money.

It took me a long time to decide what to wear. I grew bored with my favourite clothes and craved new ones, along with bags and shoes. I realised that the concept of having a uniform is quite logical; it saves time, energy and even money.

Mark Zuckerberg wears the same grey T-shirt every day, treating it like his uniform. Minimalism is all about simplifying your life and focusing on what truly matters to you. For Mark Zuckerberg, that means simplifying his wardrobe so he can spend less time worrying about what to wear and more time focusing on the things that truly inspire him, such as building Facebook and connecting people worldwide.

When you have fewer choices to make, you free up mental space to focus on what truly matters. For instance, instead of stressing over what to wear each day, Mark Zuckerberg can simply grab his grey T-shirt and jeans, allowing him to get on with his day. This approach removes one decision from his routine, which is a huge relief in our busy lives.

However, minimalism is not just about clothing – it is also a mindset. It involves making intentional choices about spending your time, energy and resources to live a more meaningful and fulfilling life.

For example, let us say you decide to declutter your room and get rid of all the items you never use. Suddenly, you have more space to breathe and a clearer understanding of what is important to you. As you simplify your physical space, you may find that your mind feels clearer and more focused.

Alternatively, you might choose to cut down on your commitments and say no to things that do not align with your values or priorities. As a result, you gain more time and energy to devote to what truly excites you – whether that is spending time with friends and family, pursuing your passions or simply enjoying a quiet moment of solitude.

Minimalism is all about simplifying your life so you can focus on what really matters. By embracing minimalism as a mindfulness practice, you can create more space for the things that bring you joy and fulfilment.

My dad introduced the concept of 'selective minimalism'. He said, 'I understand that everyone has their preferences.' To illustrate this, he used my mom as an example. She had a large collection of wallets and handbags that she was fond of. He emphasised that it is perfectly acceptable to collect one or two things that you truly love. However, aside from those items, it is important to let go of things that do not hold much value for you.

I pondered this thought for months to identify what truly mattered to me and what did not. To be honest, it was a challenging process. I did not want to discard the things that I had accumulated. I even collected empty perfume bottles, boarding passes and receipts. Eventually, I realised that most of these items were just clutter with no real value. I have a fondness for stationery, so I decided to focus on that category. It has been years now, and I do not hoard anything other than stationery.

Selective minimalism is similar to being a picky eater; instead of choosing foods, you choose what you allow into your life – whether those are physical belongings, commitments or distractions. It is about being intentional about what you bring into your space and schedule, focusing only on the things that genuinely add value and joy to your life.

Imagine your life as a backpack. You only have so much space in your backpack, right? So you want to make sure you fill it with the things that matter most to you because, ultimately, you are the one who has to carry it. That's when selective minimalism comes into play.

For example, let us say you really want to buy the latest model of the iPhone. Instead of making an impulsive purchase just because it is trendy and everyone else is buying it, take a moment and ask yourself: 'Do I really need this? Will it genuinely enhance my life in a meaningful way?'

If the answer is no, then skip the purchase and save both your space and your money for something that really matters to you.

Selective minimalism is also about setting boundaries and saying no to things that do not align with your values or priorities. Maybe you frequently receive invitations to events or requests to take on additional projects at work. Instead of saying yes to everything and risking burnout, you can embrace selective minimalism by choosing only the opportunities that truly resonate with you and bring you closer to your goals.

But here is the thing: selective minimalism is not about deprivation or saying no to everything. It is about being intentional and deliberate with your choices. Being mindful of what you allow into your life creates space for what truly matters to you. Ultimately, it is about creating a life that is filled with purpose, meaning and joy – without the burden of unnecessary distractions.

Recently, I learned about a new concept called 'digital minimalism', and I have my brother to thank for it. Unlike many, he does not have 1,000 screenshots saved in his phone, 2,000 photos from our recent family trips or 5,000 selfies. He does not keep 50 apps on his phone just because he downloaded them once and has not got around to deleting the ones he does not use. His phone is clutter-free. This is digital minimalism.

Digital minimalism is about simplifying your digital life by reducing the clutter on your devices – such as phones, computers, hard disks or memory cards. It involves reducing your screen time and focusing on what truly matters to you.

Digital minimalism is akin to decluttering your digital space, allowing more room to engage in meaningful activities and fostering genuine connections. Rather than mindlessly scrolling through social media or spending countless hours on your devices, digital minimalism encourages a more intentional use of technology.

It is a misconception that minimalism requires you to give up everything you own and live like a monk. While some people may practise extreme minimalism, I do not advocate for it. Although it is a personal choice, I believe in enjoying life to the fullest while being mindful of the things I own and the environment around me. That is why I prefer selective minimalism.

Eight Tips to Start with Minimalism for Beginners

- Follow my three-month declutter rule.
- Choose quality over quantity.
- Before you buy anything, consider whether it is a need or a want; skip the hasty 'wants'.
- Invest in experiences over assets.
- Use and appreciate what you have.
- Upcycle things.
- Repeat your clothes, even the party ones.
- Select only two or three things you choose to keep; let go of the rest.

Your Mindful Night Routine

Surprisingly, your night routine plays a significant role in mindful living, which is directly linked to your success and personal growth.

In the hustle and bustle of modern life, it is easy to overlook the importance of a good night routine. However, the moments before we fall asleep hold immense power over our overall well-being and quality of life.

A carefully crafted night routine is not just about brushing your teeth and getting into bed – it is a deliberate practice that sets the stage for restful sleep, improved mood and enhanced productivity throughout the day.

A good night routine is not just a luxury – it is a necessity for optimal health, well-being and, most important, mindful living.

In our fast-paced, chaotic world, where we are surrounded by noises like stress and distractions, taking time for a night routine helps restore balance in our lives. Moreover, studies show that quality sleep improves your ability to learn new information, enhances decision-making, boosts creativity and increases productivity.

Believe it or not, a good night routine can work wonders for your sleep. Engaging in calming activities before bed, such as reading or meditating, signals to your body that it is time to relax and prepare for sleep. As a result, you will fall asleep more easily and enjoy better sleep throughout the night.

So what can you do to create a perfect night routine?

Begin by disconnecting from screens at least an hour before bedtime. Put away your phone, tablet and computer to reduce exposure to blue light, which can interfere with your body's natural sleep-wake cycle.

Take a few moments to reflect on your day with gratitude. Consider writing in a journal about three things you are thankful for or moments that brought you joy. Reflecting on positive experiences can foster a sense of contentment and well-being.

Engage in a gentle stretching or yoga routine to release tension from your body and calm your mind. Focus on deep, mindful breaths as you move through each stretch or pose, allowing yourself to fully relax and let go of the day's stresses.

Enjoy a warm bath or shower to cleanse your body and promote relaxation. You can add soothing essential oils, such as lavender or chamomile, to enhance the calming effects. Allow yourself to fully immerse in the sensations of warmth and comfort.

Pamper your skin with a nourishing and mindful skincare routine. Use gentle, natural products and take your time to massage them into your skin with care and attention. Focus on the sensations and scents, allowing yourself to fully indulge in this self-care ritual. You can also prepare a cup of herbal tea, such as chamomile or peppermint, to help relax your body and mind. Sip slowly and mindfully, savouring the warmth and flavour of the tea as it soothes your senses.

Wind down with a calming activity, such as reading a book or practising meditation. Choose uplifting and inspiring literature or a guided meditation that promotes relaxation and mindfulness. Allow yourself to fully immerse in the present moment, letting go of any lingering worries or distractions.

Before you drift off to sleep, take a moment to express gratitude for the day and set intentions for the following day. Visualise positive outcomes and use affirmations to guide your mindset as you transition into sleep.

Ensure your sleep environment is comfortable and conducive to restorative sleep. Dim the lights, adjust the room temperature and create a tranquil atmosphere that promotes relaxation. Consider using calming sounds or white noise to drown out any external disturbances.

If you are married or have a partner with whom you share a bed, consider practising mindful intimacy before sleep. Mindful intimacy involves spending quality time together in a calm and loving manner. This can include hugging, cuddling or softly talking to each other. Engaging in these activities helps both of you feel happy and relaxed, making it easier to fall asleep. Being close to your partner can reduce stress and make you feel safe. This helps you sleep better and feel more connected to each other.

As you settle into bed, practise mindful breathing to calm your mind and prepare for sleep. Focus on the sensation of your breath as it enters and leaves your body, allowing yourself to become fully present in the moment.

What is my mindful night routine?

I am a nocturnal person, and I enjoy the night. In fact, as I write this book, the clock is about to strike 11:11 PM.

The saying 'Early to bed, early to rise' is a good rule, but most people like me fail to follow it – especially in this digital age and if you work independently like me.

I prefer to work on my books at night because, as I mentioned, the peace and serenity of nighttime enhances my productivity and concentration.

While researching, writing or journaling, I light a scented candle on my table or use an essential oil diffuser. I practise digital detox by disconnecting from devices at least 30 minutes before I go to sleep. So whether I am watching a movie or binge-watching a web series, I make sure to put the gadget away or turn off the television at least half an hour before bedtime.

I start my nighttime routine by cleaning my face, brushing my teeth, applying lotion and massaging my feet. When I lie down to sleep, I begin chanting mantras, switchwords or visualising my dreams and goals until I drift off.

In the past, I used to listen to songs or podcasts before bedtime, but I realised that this often had a negative effect on the brain. Not all podcast episodes are positive, and not every song has uplifting lyrics. I remember listening to a particular podcast at night, and in one episode, they discussed paranormal experiences. The stories they shared replayed in my mind, leading to nightmares that left me feeling heavy and exhausted.

You cannot develop a habit around something that you cannot control. I wouldn't recommend making a routine of watching YouTube videos or listening to podcasts before sleep. Many people listen to their horoscopes or tarot readings for the next day before going to bed, which is problematic because even one negative sentence can ruin an entire day. How?

I have already explained how the brain functions and responds to negative signs and signals. When you start to feel sleepy, your brain's ability to grasp and learn information is heightened compared to during the daytime when you are more active. This is the moment when your brain switches from a conscious to a subconscious state. So if you expose yourself to negative content or anything that causes fear or anxiety at this time, those feelings can linger and manifest in your life.

Maybe you have experienced something similar. When you read or listen to a horoscope that predicts a fight with someone, you might find yourself thinking about it constantly until it eventually occurs. Even if it doesn't happen at the predicted time, your anticipation may contribute to making it a reality.

So the last thing you engage in before falling asleep should be something you can fully control. This is why I recommend journaling or listening to sleep meditations or subliminals.

Your Mindful Morning Routine

A mindful morning routine is just as important as a mindful night routine. A thoughtful start to your day can set a positive tone, helping you feel grounded, focused and ready to tackle whatever comes your way.

While it is often recommended to wake up early, between 4:30 AM and 6:30 AM, I understand that modern realities and lifestyles can make this difficult. Adapting to such an early routine can be challenging for many people, including those with jobs or students. Personally, I only wake up this early for specific reasons, like scheduled morning travel or an early morning meeting.

But at least do not wake up at 1 PM, as that is not a healthy choice. So how do you decide when to wake up?

Research suggests that you should wake up at least 60–90 minutes before starting work. This gives you enough time to shake off any grogginess and prepare for the day ahead. It can also help you avoid feeling rushed and allow you to start your day with a sense of calm.

The first thing you should do after waking up is brush your teeth and wash your face with fresh water.

Afterwards, you can prepare your morning drink – whether it is milk, tea or coffee – and take a moment to be present. If you have houseplants, spend some time with them. Gardening is one of the most powerful mindful morning practices. It benefits you not only physically and mentally but also spiritually.

In addition to this, practise breathing exercises. One simple breathing exercise is to close your eyes and inhale slowly through your nose while counting to four. Then, exhale slowly through your mouth, while counting to six. Repeat this several times, allowing yourself to relax and calm your mind.

Consider incorporating gentle stretching or yoga poses into your morning routine. This helps wake up your body while promoting flexibility and mobility. Focus on slow, mindful movements and how your body feels as you stretch and release tension.

If you prefer, hitting the gym or going for a jog, walk or fitness class in the morning is also a great option.

Additionally, I recommend maintaining a morning journal. In it, you can write affirmations, express gratitude, outline your daily goals, identify priority tasks and visualise your future.

If you do not have a journal, consider starting your day with visualisation. Spend a few moments visualising your goals and intentions for the day ahead. Picture yourself accomplishing tasks with ease, feeling confident and focused, and handling challenges with grace and resilience. Visualising success can help you cultivate a positive mindset for the day. A vision board is a great tool for this.

After your visualisation, enjoy a healthy breakfast mindfully, paying attention to the taste, texture and aroma of your food. Take your time to chew slowly and savour each bite, fully immersing yourself in the experience of eating.

In addition to this, consider incorporating prayer. Regardless of your religion, caste, creed or culture, you likely believe in some form of higher divine power to whom you can pray. Dedicate at least ten minutes to expressing gratitude and praying.

The most important aspect of your morning routine is a digital detox. Start your day by avoiding screens and electronics for the first hour after waking up.

Earlier, I had a habit of checking my phone the moment I woke up, but I have since changed that. Now, I either check the time or place my phone on a table far from my bed and do not touch it until I have finished my coffee and journaling.

Remember, the key to a mindful morning routine is consistency and intentionality. By incorporating these practices into your daily routine, you can cultivate greater mindfulness, presence and well-being in your life. Feel free to adjust and personalise this routine to suit your preferences and schedule, but whatever you choose to start, try to stick to it.

Find Your Soul Food

Just as sunlight, water and care are essential for the growth of tender plants, your soul also requires nourishment. It thrives on experiences that bring you joy, peace and a deeper sense of presence.

One key aspect of soul food for mindfulness is spending time in nature. Nature has a magical way of grounding us, helping us feel more connected to the world around us and reminding us of life's beauty and wonder.

Soul food can be anything that brings you inner contentment and satisfaction, providing you with peace of mind.

Nature is one of the greatest sources of soul food. Ever wondered why mountains, jungles, rivers and beaches instantly make you feel happy? They are your soul food. Sometimes, you might have little interest in learning about the history or culture of a place, yet you visit purely for its beauty, as in Kashmir or Kerala.

Being surrounded by nature calms our minds and uplifts our spirits. Being amid nature is like therapy or a spa, where you return feeling revived and rejuvenated.

My dad used to take us to Nainital every three months during the last five years of his life, spending at least two days there each time. At times, we felt bored and chose to skip travelling with him.

When I asked why he kept visiting the same place, pointing out that we could spend the same amount of money to explore a new destination, he replied, 'Indeed we can do that, which is why I plan trips to other places too. But Nainital is my soul food.'

Soul food is not just about nature or travel; it can be anything. It is your personal diet chart for the soul, and you decide what works best for you.

Soul food can include activities like meditation, practising music, going to the gym, journaling, pursuing a hobby, scrapbooking, talking to an elderly person, watching a play, enjoying a long, relaxing bath with essential oil diffusers, inhaling your favourite perfume for 20 to 30 seconds, walking barefoot on grass or simply watching the stars and the moon. It can be anything.

Body Scan

A body scan is a mindfulness practice that involves focusing your attention on different parts of your body. During this practice, you notice any sensations, tension or feelings without passing judgement. It is similar to taking a tour of your body but with your mind instead of your feet!

To begin, find a comfortable spot to lie down, like your bed or a cosy mat. Start by taking some deep breaths to help you relax. Then, gradually shift your focus to different body parts, starting from your toes or the top of your head, whichever you prefer.

Now, here is the fun part! As you shift your attention, take a moment to check in with each part of your body, almost like saying, 'Hey, how are you doing down there, toes?' Notice any sensations you feel – maybe your toes are tingling, your legs feel heavy or your tummy is rumbling because you are hungry!

There is no right or wrong way to feel; you simply observe whatever is happening without judging it.

As you continue scanning your body, you might notice areas that feel tense or relaxed, warm or cool, comfortable or uncomfortable. And that is totally okay! The key is to observe whatever you are feeling without trying to change it.

The great thing about a body scan is that it helps you become more aware of how your body feels in the present moment. It is like giving your body extra attention and care, similar to how you would care for a pet or a plant. And guess what? It can help you relax, reduce stress and feel grounded and calm.

The body scan is important. I recommend doing a body scan at least once a month. If you notice anything that feels off, focus on that area and work on improving it.

You might be curious how this is relevant to shooing the noises. In fact, it makes us more aware of our internal noises, like an unhealthy or flawed body, which might lead to feelings of insecurity.

There is a difference in perspective. While you may think otherwise, maintaining a healthy and sound body is essential for a successful life. True success comes from achieving a perfect balance between your mind, soul and body.

Imagine experiencing severe hair fall or persistent knee pain. Would you be able to deliver your best work and reach your highest potential while dealing with these issues? Absolutely not! Such distractions would keep you from focusing on your purpose.

A body scan is one of the best ways to bring balance to your life and help you achieve your dreams and desires.

Mindful Eating

Many of you either watch television or use your phone while having your meal. This is one of the unhealthiest ways to eat. I will not lie; even I used to do the same until a few years ago.

Mindful eating involves being aware of 'what' you eat and 'how' you eat it. Imagine your favourite meal – the colours, the smells and the delicious taste. Mindful eating is about giving your full attention to that experience.

Most of us can still recall the taste of a vegetable our mothers or grandmothers cooked for us. How? Because decades ago, we sat down and ate without distractions. Our focus was entirely on the food and every single bite was etched in our memories.

You must have heard an elder say, '*Isiliye khana sharir ko nahi lagta,*' implying that we do not absorb nutrients from our meals because we are distracted while eating. They are right. We often do not practise mindful eating, so we miss out on its benefits.

When you sit down for a meal, try not to rush. Take your time to enjoy each bite. Taste the flavours, feel the textures and immerse yourself in the food. It is like a mini adventure for your taste buds!

Mindful eating is not just about the food; it is also about how you feel. Pay attention to when you are hungry and when you are full. Your body communicates these signals and listening to them is essential.

Now, let me ask you – did your school have a tradition of saying a small prayer before lunch?

This practice is one of the major aspects of mindful eating: gratitude.

Expressing gratitude before eating means taking a moment to thank those who contributed to the meal we are about to enjoy. It is a way to show appreciation for the delicious food in front of us.

Before you start eating, take a moment to appreciate all the people who contributed to bringing this food to your table – the farmers who grew the crops, the workers who harvested them and the person who prepared the meal. Not just them but also your God, nature and the work that enabled you to bring this food to the table.

By practising gratitude before eating, we show respect not only for the food itself but also for the people and the Earth that produced it. It is like saying, 'Thank you for this wonderful meal!'

Sometimes, life can get incredibly busy. We eat in a rush or get distracted by the television. Practising mindful eating encourages us to eliminate distractions. Turn off the TV, put away your phone and focus entirely on your meal.

Although it might seem unusual at first, being mindful about your food can enhance your eating experience while also providing physical benefits such as improved digestion, better weight management and enhanced mental well-being.

Mind Your Words

I want you to think of a word that triggers strong emotions, like anger or disappointment, especially when it is said by someone you love. Now consider this: when someone tells you, 'I am proud of you' or 'I love you', do you stop to think before smiling? No, that smile is a reflex that comes naturally from positivity.

This reaction is rooted in the idea that words carry frequency – low and high.

I once came across a thought-provoking quote by Bruce Lee: 'Do not speak negatively about yourself, even as a joke. Your body does not know the difference. Words are energy and they cast spells; that is why they are called spelling. Change how you speak about yourself, and you can change your life.' These words resonated with me.

We must be mindful of our words, especially when talking about ourselves, whether to others or ourselves. This practice is known as 'mindful speaking'.

Mindful speaking means being careful about the words we use and understanding how they affect us and those around us. It is like being aware of the magic our words carry and using them in a way that uplifts rather than harms us.

Many of you may be familiar with mantras, switchwords or even affirmations. When chanted, these magical phrases can transform our lives because they carry energy. Words can bypass all channels and filters and directly affect our minds.

I have observed some people, out of modesty, say things like: 'Oh no, I am not a big deal!', 'Welcome to my small, humble home', 'I am not rich; I am just like you', 'I do not think I am that great a singer'. This is despite the fact that they may be accomplished, own large homes, possess wealth or be renowned as talented singers.

People often conflate being grounded and staying humble with using negative affirmations. They believe that such sentences make them appear humble and grounded.

No, it does not. In fact, when you use negative language, it can lead others to feel that you are making fun of them. Negative affirmations can take away the positive experiences or rewards you have earned.

I am from Kanpur and here in my city, if you ask someone how work is going, they may reply with something like '*Bas baba ki kripa hai*' or '*Chal raha hai apke ashirwad se*'. I found it a smart way of responding modestly while not affirming anything negative.

It is important to be mindful of what we say. Using positive words and affirmations can uplift us and those around us.

People often believe they look cool when using swear words, especially in Delhi. They claim they do not mean it and that it is just slang, but in reality, this creates a circle of negativity around them. It is not cool to use profanity.

Whatever energy we emit, whether through our words or other forms of expression, comes back to us multiplied.

So remember to speak kindly to yourself and others. Choose words that uplift you and spread positive vibes. It is not just about what we say but also about the energy we project into the world.

Next time someone appreciates you, accept that compliment with positivity. Also, think twice before you speak, especially about yourself.

Prompts for Mindfulness

- Take a few moments to focus on your breath. Notice the sensation of air entering and leaving your body.
- Pay attention to what is happening in the present moment without judgement or attachment to the past or future.
- Tune into your surroundings using your senses. Notice the sights, sounds, smells, tastes and textures around you.
- Take time each day to appreciate the little things in life. Reflect on what you are thankful for.
- Embrace things as they are, even if they are challenging. Practise accepting yourself and others without judgement.
- Release the need to control everything. Allow things to unfold naturally, trusting the process.
- Whether you are eating, walking or talking to someone, give your full attention to the present moment.
- Schedule short breaks throughout your day to pause, breathe and reset your focus.
- Treat yourself with kindness and compassion, just as you would a good friend.
- Remember, mindfulness is a skill that grows with practice. Be patient with yourself and keep showing up.

14

The Perfect Balance: Mind, Body and Soul

Throughout this entire book, I have discussed various noises, such as distractions, barriers and blockages, that pull us in all directions.

But when we find that sweet balance within ourselves, we can navigate through the noise and emerge even stronger.

Our journey begins with the mind – the epicentre of our thoughts, emotions and beliefs. Picture your mind as a bustling marketplace filled with chatter and activity. In this marketplace, it is easy to get swept away by the noises – the doubts, fears and worries that cloud our judgement and hold us back.

But guess what? We can shoo away the noises and cultivate a sense of calm and clarity within our minds.

One of our most powerful tools is mindfulness – a practice that encourages us to be fully present in the moment, without judgement or attachment to the past or future. As discussed earlier, mindfulness allows us to observe our thoughts and emotions with curiosity and compassion rather than becoming tangled in them.

Ram Dass, an American spiritual guru, psychologist and writer, once said, 'The quieter you become, the more you can hear.'

By quieting the noise of our minds through mindfulness, we create space for clarity, insight and wise decision-making.

However, achieving balance involves more than just taming the mind; it is also about nurturing our bodies, the vessels that carry us through life's adventures.

Our bodies are temples that deserve love, care and respect. When we neglect our bodies, consume junk food, skip exercise or even hold on to negative energies and thought patterns, we disrupt the delicate balance within ourselves.

So how do we care for our bodies in a way that promotes balance and vitality? It is all about nourishing ourselves with wholesome foods, staying active and listening to our bodies' cues. Eating a balanced diet filled with fruits, vegetables, whole grains and lean proteins fuels our bodies with the nutrients they need to thrive. And when it comes to exercise, it is not about running marathons or hitting the gym for hours on end; it is about finding activities that we enjoy and that make us feel alive, whether it is dancing, hiking or practising yoga.

But here is the thing: achieving balance is not just about the mind and body but also about nurturing our souls – the essence of who we are. Our souls crave connection, meaning and purpose. They yearn for experiences that nourish our spirits and ignite our passions.

It starts with connecting to something greater than ourselves – whether through nature, spirituality, art or service to others. Spending time in nature, for example, can be incredibly nourishing for the soul, reminding us of the beauty and wonder of the world around us. Engaging in spiritual practices, such as meditation, prayer or mindfulness, can also provide solace and guidance on our journey.

And let us not forget about the power of community and connection.

Surrounding ourselves with supportive friends, family and mentors can uplift our spirits, provide encouragement and remind us that we are not alone on this journey. As the saying goes, 'Alone we can do so little; together we can do so much.'

But you see, striking the perfect balance in your life is not that tough either, and it is not also necessary to turn into a saint and only practise meditation. It can be achieved in a fun way, too, simply by adopting a hobby.

According to a report published by Harvard Health, people with hobbies report better health, more happiness, higher satisfaction in life and fewer symptoms of depression.[1]

---

[1] www. health.harvard.edu/mind-and-mood/having-a-hobby-tied-to-happiness-and-well-being

3-2-1 Rule for a Balanced Life

I personally follow this rule to bring balance to my life. This daily practice has changed my life in a big way. When I was going through the toughest phase of my life after losing both of my parents within a span of one year, I was just running mentally to seek answers, while physically, I looked lost.

I remember sitting in the temple, almost blank, not knowing the whats and whys until someone asked me, 'Are you okay?'

It was the temple's priest.

'Yes, I am fine!' I said.

'You do not look like it,' he observed.

I felt he could gaze straight into my soul. I was not okay. He was right.

'I am missing my parents. They left me.'

He immediately understood that the reason was grief. 'Beta, you cannot bring them back, but they are now alive in your heart and soul. Being lost and sad is not just making you suffer but also them as they are a part of your now.'

'I do not know what to do. I have lost all hope and motivation to do anything in life.' I could not stop crying.

'You need to heal yourself,' he explained.

'How?'

'You have lost balance. Just bring balance to your life. A sound body, mind and soul will help you overcome all the blockages and barriers in life. The void created by your parents will never be filled, but it is up to you how to deal with it. Grief is the biggest noise in our lives. We need to face it, accept it and heal it.'

This was my first step towards healing myself and bouncing back in life.

I have been following this 3-2-1 rule for a balanced life since then. No matter how tired or unwilling I feel, I force myself to do it. It is like homework to me: if I do not do it, I punish myself with something like not drinking my favourite drink for the day or not watching the next episode of a web series.

The Perfect Balance: Mind, Body and Soul

The 3-2-1 rule is simple:
- Do 3 things for your mind.
- Do 2 things for your body.
- Do 1 thing for your soul.

And you have to do it every day, without missing a single day, until it becomes a habit.

Some ideas on what you can do for your mind:
- Read something every day (newspaper, book or magazine).
- Solve a puzzle.
- Reduce your screen time.
- Learn something new.
- Take a walk and get some fresh air.
- Meditate.

Some ideas on what you can do for your body:
- Eat healthily, including more greens and fruits.
- Curtail sugar intake.
- Include physical activity (walking, running, gym, dance, yoga, stretching or cycling).
- Take care of your skin.
- Sleep at least 8 hours every 24 hours.

Some ideas on what you can do for your soul:
- Travel.
- Start working on your passion project.
- Do acts of kindness.
- Declutter.
- Start saying no to things that do not align with your goals.
- Allow yourself to relax.
- Spend some time in nature.
- Diffuse essential oils; have aromatherapy evenings.

15

Your Greatest Noise: Your Comfort Zone

Your growth in life depends entirely on your limits, which act like invisible walls surrounding us, defining what we believe we can and cannot do. They represent the boundaries we set for ourselves based on our beliefs, fears and experiences.

But what if I told you these limits are not as solid as they seem? What if breaking through them could open up a world of possibilities and opportunities?

The first step to breaking through these limits is to shoo your greatest noise: your 'comfort zone'.

Comfort zones hold us back. They prevent us from growing, learning and experiencing new things. When we stay within our comfort zones, we miss out on opportunities for personal and professional growth.

To step out of your comfort zone, you need to develop a success mindset. Achieving a success mindset requires a shift in your perception of things. There is a saying that goes, 'We cannot solve our problems with the same level of thinking that created them.' This is so true. To find solutions to your problems, you need to switch to a different frequency in your thought process and adopt a different perspective.

Picture this: you are relaxing on your favourite couch, wrapped in a cosy blanket, watching your favourite TV show. It feels safe, warm and incredibly comfortable. That is what your comfort zone looks like.

However, the truth is that staying in that snug spot forever will not lead to personal growth or success. Not at all.

But here is where things get interesting. While your comfort zone may feel warm and fuzzy, it is also the place where growth takes a nap. Staying within those comfortable boundaries means you are not challenging yourself, not pushing your limits and not venturing into the unknown.

So why should you leave the comfort of that snug bubble?

Well, let me tell you why – there is a whole world out there waiting to be explored! Stepping out of your comfort zone is like opening the door to a grand adventure. It is about trying new things, meeting new people and taking risks that could lead to amazing experiences.

Sure, it might feel scary at first. Stepping into the unknown often feels that way. But guess what? That is where the magic happens! It is in those moments that you discover things about yourself you never knew existed. It is where you learn to embrace challenges, conquer fears and grow into the best version of yourself.

For instance, an introvert may feel uncomfortable attending a networking event where potential investors are present. A shy person might hesitate to audition for a dance reality show even if they have a chance to win the trophy. Similarly, a late riser may avoid joining a morning yoga class because waking up at 6 AM feels too daunting. All of these examples highlight the limitations of one's comfort zone.

You cannot achieve something extraordinary by sticking to ordinary approaches. As humans, we are often programmed to operate within our comfort zones. We tend to compromise on our goals simply because we are too lazy or scared to step outside those comfort zones.

If you have a goal – whether personal or professional – it is essential to challenge your comfort zone. Taking this step involves significant risk, and I will not say it will be easy, but it will be worth it.

The greatest and most successful people in history have often been significant risk-takers. Bill Gates, Steve Jobs, Elon Musk, Henry

Ford, Nelson Mandela, Dr Abdul Kalam, Nambi Narayanan, Lata Mangeshkar and Kapil Dev are just a few of the remarkable figures who have made history. These individuals were not afraid to take risks, push their limits and step out of their comfort zones.

Among all these inspiring stories of pushing boundaries and achieving great success, my personal favourite is that of M.S. Dhoni, the Indian cricketer, who is considered one of the finest in his field.

Even when he worked as a ticket examiner (TTE), he prioritised practising cricket whenever possible. He sometimes skipped meals to ensure he could practise. Balancing his job and his passion for cricket was challenging, but Dhoni was determined not to give up. He pushed his limits and stepped out of his comfort zone. He practised hard, even after long days at work, and his dedication paid off. M.S. Dhoni made his international cricket debut for India in a One Day International (ODI) match against Bangladesh on 23 December 2004. He became the captain of the Indian cricket team in ODIs in September 2007. Under his captaincy, India won the ICC Cricket World Cup in 2011.

Successful people are not born into success; they make it happen. They do not procrastinate or allow delays; they value their time and energy. They understand that their goals will never come to fruition if they do not take action.

I would like to share an insightful concept: the 5-second rule, introduced by Mel Robbins. She suggests that if you want to act on a goal, you must physically make a move within the first 5 seconds or your brain will kill it.

It is a powerful observation. It actually helped me deal with procrastination and laziness. You must try it too!

Affirmations for Stepping Out of the Comfort Zone

- I am ready for new challenges.
- I embrace discomfort as a sign of growth.
- I am capable of more than I think.
- I welcome change and opportunities.

- I thrive outside my comfort zone.
- I believe in my ability to adapt.
- I am open to new experiences.
- I am courageous and resilient.
- I push my limits and grow stronger.
- I trust in my ability to succeed.

16

Self-Worth and Acceptance

MANY OF US OFTEN confuse self-worth with the possessions we own or the achievements we accumulate. We are constantly bombarded with messages suggesting that our value is determined by the number of likes on social media, the brands we wear or the cars we drive. But let me tell you, self-worth goes much deeper than material possessions and external validation.

Do you only feel worthy when you have the latest gadgets and designer clothes, when you go on a luxury trip, buy a car or reach a certain number of followers online?

Yes, you do! But it is wrong.

True self-worth comes from within. It involves recognising your inherent value as a human being, regardless of your achievements.

As the author Nathaniel Branden aptly stated, 'Self-esteem is the reputation we acquire with ourselves.'

You are valuable simply because you exist.

There is no need to prove your worth to anyone, not even to yourself. Your worth is not determined by your job title, your bank account balance or the number of trophies you have. It is about embracing your uniqueness, your flaws and your imperfections.

According to research, people who base their self-worth on external factors, like wealth or appearance, are more likely to experience anxiety, depression and low self-esteem. Conversely, those who cultivate self-acceptance and recognise their intrinsic worth tend to lead happier, more fulfilling lives.

Self-worth comes with acceptance.

Self-Worth and Acceptance

Acceptance is not about resigning yourself to your circumstances or passively enduring life's challenges. It involves acknowledging reality and embracing both the light and shadows within ourselves. Accept your imperfections, embrace your flaws and take ownership of your reality.

When we own our reality and accept our imperfections, we permit ourselves to be human. As the renowned psychologist Carl Rogers once said, 'The curious paradox is that when I accept myself just as I am, then I can change.'

Acceptance means making peace with your past, forgiving yourself for your mistakes and letting go of unrealistic expectations. It involves understanding that you are a work in progress – a masterpiece in the making – complete with flaws and imperfections that make you uniquely beautiful.

In this world filled with noises – be it societal expectations, comparison traps or self-doubt – finding self-acceptance can feel like navigating through a dense forest.

How do we shoo away the noises and clear the path with self-worth and acceptance?

It starts with self-reflection and introspection.

Take a moment to tune out the external chatter and listen to the whispers of your heart.

Consider your values, your passions, your dreams.

What makes you feel truly alive and fulfilled?

Next, practise self-care and self-compassion.

As I mentioned, start treating yourself with the same kindness and understanding you would offer to someone you love dearly.

Nurture your mind, body and soul with activities that uplift and rejuvenate you.

Remember, you are worthy of love, respect and happiness – simply because you are. There is no other legitimate reason. Your very existence is the fundamental reason for deserving all of these good things.

Surround yourself with people who uplift you and celebrate your strengths. Build relationships based on authenticity, trust and mutual respect. Let go of toxic connections that drain your energy and diminish your sense of self-worth.

Celebrate your victories, no matter how small, and learn from your setbacks with grace and resilience.

Understand that life is filled with a series of ups and downs. It is a beautiful tapestry woven with threads of joy, sorrow, love and loss.

As the poet Maya Angelou once said, 'You alone are enough. You have nothing to prove to anybody.'

Your worth is not determined by the noise of the world but by the quiet whispers of your soul.

When you truly accept yourself, flaws and all, you can identify your true strengths. Think about it: you cannot address a problem if you do not even know the problem, right? Makes sense?

I remember overhearing a conversation between two strangers while waiting for my taxi. We were standing outside a five-star hotel. I had just concluded a workshop while these two boys, I assume, came out of a cafe.

The valet got one of the boys' cars.

The other boy was unaware that his friend had bought this cool car. 'OMG, you bought an Aston Martin DB12?'

'Yes, last month itself!'

'Oh, can I drive it, please? I read about this in an auto magazine. It is like a dream car. This is badass!'

The car owner responded with a simple 'thank you', experiencing a sense of pride, as if he were the car itself, receiving appreciation.

We often forget that we are not our possessions. When someone compliments our assets, like cars, houses or gadgets, we tend to take it personally. We start to feel that these things enhance our worth. But the truth is, they do not. They are merely items that we can afford to buy.

Your self-worth is defined by your brain. It is defined by your behaviour, your sense of compassion, your kindness and your perspective on life. All this stems from acceptance. You need to know who you truly are and what noises you need to mute. Once you begin to realise your self-worth, you will naturally build confidence, leading to an increase in your self-esteem.

There are many ways to realise your self-worth and develop self-acceptance, but my favourite is the Ho'oponopono prayer.

The Ho'oponopono prayer is a Hawaiian prayer used to cultivate forgiveness and resolve conflicts, either with ourselves or with others. If you search the internet, you will see many people use it for reconciliation with their ex-partners and for improving relationships. While it certainly works wonders in those situations – after all, it is a prayer – I have personally found that it is especially effective in fostering self-love and acceptance.

Imagine it as cleaning a messy room in your house. The Ho'oponopono prayer helps tidy up your mind and heart, creating space for more positive thoughts and feelings. When we feel better about ourselves, our sense of self-worth grows stronger.

Earlier, we discussed the noises like self-doubt, grudges, guilt, despair, anger and complexes. By practising the Ho'oponopono prayer for ourselves, we can eliminate these noises from our lives, thereby building a stronger sense of self-worth.

So what is the Ho'oponopono prayer?

It involves repeating four key phrases:
- I am sorry
- Please forgive me
- Thank you
- I love you

These phrases can be repeated either silently or aloud, directed towards oneself, others or a higher power, depending on the context.

Mirror Technique

I practise the Ho'oponopono prayer but with a twist. This is a little secret I am sharing with you.

Whenever I feel lost and low, when my confidence is shaking or when I question my self-worth, I stand in front of the mirror and say the following phrases:
- I am sorry
- Please forgive me
- I love you
- <affirmation>
- Thank you

I repeat this for five to ten minutes, looking straight into my eyes, and then drink a glass of fresh water.

The affirmation is the main purpose of my practice. For example, if I am feeling sad, I might say, 'You are very happy.' If I feel a lack of love in my life, I would say, 'You radiate love; you attract love.' Sometimes, I keep it simple and say, 'You are amazing! You are the best!'

This practice always uplifts me. If you do not believe it, give it a try tonight!

Inspiring Quotes

You were born to be real, not to be perfect. You are here to be you, not to live someone else's life.

— Ralph Marston

The only person who can pull me down is myself, and I'm not going to let myself pull me down anymore.

— C. JoyBell C.

To be beautiful means to be yourself. You don't need to be accepted by others. You need to accept yourself.

— Thich Nhat Hanh

You yourself, as much as anybody in the entire universe, deserve your love and affection.

— Buddha

17

The Science of Habits

HABIT PLAYS A CRUCIAL role in shaping our lives, both positively and negatively. Bad habits are the loudest noise that affect us on many levels. While you may already understand what a habit is, it is essential to explore how it is formed and how to break it, which is the focus of this chapter.

Have you ever wondered why you instinctively reach for a chocolate bar when stressed or feel compelled to check your phone as soon as you wake up? These actions can be traced back to the interaction of cues, routines and rewards that shape our behaviours.

Cues

First, let us talk about cues.

Cues are triggers in our environment that prompt us to engage in certain behaviours. These cues can come in many forms – such as a time of day, a specific location or even an emotional state. For example, when you wake up in the morning, you may not even think about it; you simply go to the washbasin, grab your toothbrush and start brushing your teeth. Here, morning is the cue.

Routines

Next, let us discuss routines.

Routines are the specific behaviours or actions we take in response to cues. They represent our habits – the actions we perform automatically, often without conscious thought. For example, when you feel stressed (cue), you might instinctively reach for a chocolate bar (routine) to help improve your mood.

Rewards

Last but not least, let us talk about rewards.

Rewards are the positive outcomes or feelings we experience from engaging in a routine. They act like little treats that our brain provides to reinforce the behaviour and encourage us to do it again in the future. So when you eat that chocolate bar, you might experience a momentary boost in mood or a sense of comfort, which serves as a reward and makes you more likely to reach for it again the next time you feel stressed.

The key to habit formation lies in the relationship between these three elements. When we encounter a cue, it triggers a routine, leading to a reward. Over time, this process becomes ingrained in our brains, forming what is known as a habit loop. The more we repeat this loop, the stronger the habit becomes.

So to change your habits, you must pay attention to the cues that trigger them, the routines themselves and the rewards you receive. By identifying the cues that prompt us to engage in certain behaviours, we can interrupt the habit loop and replace old routines with new, healthier ones. By finding alternative rewards that fulfil the exact needs of our old habits, we can rewire our brains and create lasting change.

Another key concept in habit formation is habit stacking!

Habit stacking is the practice of building new habits on top of existing ones. By leveraging established routines and behaviours, we can make it easier to adopt new habits and integrate them into our daily lives. For example, if you already have a habit of brushing your teeth before bed, you could stack a new habit, such as flossing or doing a short meditation, onto that existing routine.

Habit stacking is effective because it takes advantage of the neural pathways already established in our brains. By piggybacking new habits onto familiar ones, we can create a chain of behaviours that reinforce each other and make it easier to stick to our goals.

If we talk about the neuroscience of habit formation, there are two main players: the basal ganglia and the prefrontal cortex.

The basal ganglia are a group of nuclei in the brain's centre responsible for complex processes affecting our whole body. Whenever you do something repeatedly, like brushing your teeth or riding a bike, the basal ganglia remember it and help you do it without even thinking. It is like your brain's personal assistant!

The prefrontal cortex is our brain's Big Boss, also known as the 'personality centre'. It is the most evolved region of the brain, responsible for promoting our highest-order cognitive abilities like speech formation, gaze, reasoning, planning, problem-solving, abstract thinking and habit formation. When you learn a new habit, like playing a new sport or learning to cook, the prefrontal cortex works hard to figure it all out.

So when you keep doing something repeatedly, certain parts of your brain, called neural circuits in the basal ganglia, get stronger. This happens because the connections between brain cells, called synapses, change to make the circuits more efficient. A chemical messenger in the brain called dopamine is important for this process. It is produced by specialised cells located in areas of the brain called the substantia nigra (SN) and ventral tegmental area (VTA). From there, dopamine travels to another part of the brain called the striatum, where it strengthens the connections between brain cells.

Eventually, this process makes it easier for your brain to perform a behaviour without needing to think about it too much. As a result, habits form – these are actions you do almost automatically, requiring little effort.

For example, once you learn how to ride a bike, you do not need to figure everything out again, read a user manual or seek expert help to ride it every day. You simply do it without much thought.

When you form a habit, you often associate specific situations or cues with certain actions.

When you see or smell something familiar, your brain automatically cues the associated habit.

Two key parts of the brain, the basolateral amygdala and hippocampus, help you remember the context or situation in which you develop a habit. This means they link the specific situation to the habit itself. Another part of the brain, the dorsomedial striatum, helps connect specific cues with the actions you take. These connections help you perform actions automatically when you encounter familiar cues or find yourself in familiar situations, even if you are not actively thinking about doing them.

Additionally, the brain's reward system motivates us to repeat patterns, behaviours and actions.

The primary function of the reward system is to reinforce behaviours essential for survival and well-being. When we engage in activities such as eating, socialising or accomplishing goals, the brain releases dopamine, creating feelings of pleasure and satisfaction. This positive reinforcement encourages us to repeat these behaviours, ensuring our survival and promoting our overall happiness.

Here, the important player is dopamine, which is central to our brain's reward system. We have briefly discussed dopamine earlier in this book, referring to it as the happy chemical, feel-good messenger, etc. Yes, it is this and so much more.

Dopamine serves as a motivational signal that drives us to seek rewards and take action to achieve them. When dopamine levels are low, we may experience a lack of motivation or interest in activities that we typically find rewarding. While dopamine is important for normal brain function, an imbalance in its levels can have negative consequences. Too much or too little dopamine can contribute to various mental health disorders, including depression, schizophrenia and Parkinson's disease.

Although the reward system is essential for promoting adaptive behaviours, it can also be manipulated by addictive substances and behaviours. Drugs, alcohol, gambling and other addictive activities can artificially stimulate the release of dopamine, leading to intense feelings of pleasure and reinforcing addictive behaviours. Over time, this can lead to the development of addiction, as the brain becomes increasingly dependent on the substance or behaviour to experience pleasure.

When trying to form a good habit, it is important to identify the bad habits that act as noise in your life, preventing you from understanding what is actually required for your growth.

Bad habits are like stealthy shadows that creep into our lives, often going unnoticed yet exerting a significant impact on our well-being and success. From mindlessly scrolling through social media to indulging in unhealthy eating patterns, these behaviours can subtly sabotage our goals and aspirations. The first step towards breaking free from their hold is to identify and acknowledge their presence.

Identifying bad habits requires a deliberate and introspective approach. It begins with cultivating self-awareness and paying attention to our daily behaviours. Through reflection and evaluation, we scrutinise the impact of these habits on various aspects of our lives, assessing whether they align with our goals, values and aspirations.

The most important thing is to analyse the consequences of our habits. By scrutinising the impact of our behaviours on various facets of life, we gain insight into their true cost. Habits are the building blocks of our lives. They shape our health, happiness and overall well-being. Our habits significantly influence our physical and mental health along with our relationships, productivity and overall quality of life.

For example, your diet is a crucial factor in maintaining good health. Eating a balanced diet with plenty of fruits, vegetables, whole grains and lean proteins provides essential nutrients to our bodies.

Conversely, consuming excessive amounts of processed foods, sugary snacks and high-fat meals can contribute to weight gain, high cholesterol and chronic diseases such as diabetes and heart disease.

Similarly, regular exercise is essential for keeping our bodies strong and healthy. Engaging in physical activity helps maintain a healthy weight, strengthen muscles and bones, and reduce the risk of chronic conditions like cardiovascular disease and diabetes. On the other hand, a sedentary lifestyle can lead to weight gain, muscle weakness and an increased risk of health problems.

Even substance use, including tobacco, alcohol and drugs, can have detrimental effects on physical health. Smoking, for instance, is a leading cause of preventable diseases such as lung cancer, respiratory infections and cardiovascular disorders. Excessive alcohol consumption can damage the liver, increase the risk of liver disease and contribute to addiction. Similarly, drug abuse can lead to a range of health issues, including overdose, organ damage and mental health disorders.

Similarly, our habits are directly connected to our mental health. When you are stressed or feeling overwhelmed, what do you usually do?

Some of us might turn to unhealthy habits, like staying up late, binge-watching television, eating junk food or consuming alcohol as a way to cope. This gives us momentary pleasure, escape and calmness.

On the bright side, some habits can significantly boost our mental health and increase our resilience when facing challenges. For example, cutting your screen time and keeping away your gadgets at least one hour before you sleep can be beneficial.

Habits also play an important role in shaping and sustaining our relationships. They are the building blocks of our interactions with others. They can be as simple as saying 'thank you' or as disruptive as checking our phones during conversations. These habits, whether positive or negative, influence how we communicate and relate to the people around us.

A relationship is like a delicate flower; it needs care and attention to bloom. This is where communication, empathy and mutual respect come in. These qualities are like sunshine and water for our relationships – they help them grow strong and healthy. When we communicate openly, listen with empathy and treat others with respect, we create a foundation of trust and understanding.

But not all habits are good for our relationships. Some habits, like dishonesty or a lack of empathy, can strain even the strongest bonds. Imagine if your friend always told little white lies or never took the time to understand how you were feeling. It would not feel great, right? These detrimental habits can erode trust and leave our relationships shaky and uncertain.

When people say, 'I do not care about friends, relatives, spouse, society – I just want to focus on my work, my aim, my success', they do not realise that this mindset can lead to stagnation in life.

I have previously explained how community building and having a support system help you sustain your growth and success. I am not suggesting that you rely entirely on relationships or become a people-pleaser at the expense of your own life.

Instead, I encourage you to build your universe and be conscious of how your habits affect people inside it. This awareness is important.

That is why it is important to be mindful of the habits we bring into our relationships. By being honest, empathetic and respectful, we can nurture connections built on trust and mutual support. Let us make a conscious effort to cultivate positive habits that strengthen our relationships and bring out the best in each other. After all, a little kindness and understanding can go a long way in building happy and healthy connections.

On the other hand, bad habits take away our productivity and degrade our quality of life.

A few weeks ago, while scrolling through Instagram, I came across a post that said, 'I am not lazy; I am generous because I just give others a chance to do their part as well as mine.' This post received lakhs of likes and many people agreed with it as if they felt proud of being lazy. It is wrong – plain and simple. Even the characters you see in television shows who appear lazy are often some of the most active and hardworking people in the entire unit.

Recently, I saw a photo of a fancy hotel room with a person sitting on the bed surrounded by at least seven kinds of dishes, captioned, 'Breakfast in bed, always!' My first reaction was that this was rather foolish. It sends the wrong message to young minds by suggesting that it is acceptable to wake up, stay in bed and eat breakfast without even brushing or going to the washroom. How unhygienic and illogical this is!

I grew up in an environment where my parents taught me that eating in bed is not good, not physically, not spiritually. But these days, most bad habits are dressed up as something fancy and aspirational.

Let me give another example of bad habits being shown as fancy and aspirational. Consider some of the most famous Punjabi songs, where the protagonists are seen smoking and drinking as if it were perfectly normal.

Akshay Kumar, a well-known actor in the Indian film industry, was once asked by a journalist why he goes to bed early and wakes up early. To this, he answered, 'Why should I not sleep early? Mornings are meant for waking up and getting to work. Early to bed, early to rise – this is how a routine should be. Many of us have corrupted this concept by sleeping at 12:30 or 1 AM, thinking it is cool and ridiculing those who choose to sleep early.'

This encapsulates my point. Bad habits, especially those glorified on social media, do not make you cool, enhance your lifestyle or make you successful. In fact, they degrade your life and hinder your potential for success.

For example, when you binge-watch a series until 3 AM, you end up deprived of sleep, feeling cranky the next morning, developing dark circles under your eyes and possibly arguing with someone because you are in a bad mood all day. Meanwhile, you are making the producers and owners of that app and series rich while sacrificing your own health and lifestyle. It is not free. It is costing you the most important thing of all – your well-being.

So how can you identify a bad habit?

- Pay attention to your actions and behaviours.
- Take a moment to think about whether the behaviour has negative consequences.

- Consider how the habit affects different aspects of your life.
- Compare the habit with your personal goals and values.
- Seek feedback from trusted friends, family members or a life coach.
- Identify the emotions or situations that trigger the habit.
- Look for recurring behaviours that may indicate a habit.
- Be honest with yourself about your habits and their impact.

The biggest challenge is not just identifying a bad habit but actually breaking it and moving away from it.

I know some people personally who are aware that they have a bad habit, such as alcohol consumption or smoking. They understand that they are addicted and are aware of the negative impact these habits have on their lives, yet they still struggle to break free from them.

In some cases, these habits can develop into severe addictions. If you find yourself in this situation, I recommend seeking professional help.

However, if it is just a bad habit hindering your growth, here are some tips that helped me break mine. Yes, I had my share of bad habits too, but I managed to overcome them. It took some time, but I was able to break free from all of them.

So how do you break a bad habit?

- Understand what sets off your bad habit. Is it stress, boredom or certain situations? Knowing your triggers can help you avoid them or find healthier coping methods.
- Instead of trying to stop the bad habit, replace it with a healthier alternative. For example, if you tend to stress-eat, try going for a walk or practising deep breathing instead.
- Break your habit into smaller, manageable steps. Focus on changing one small aspect at a time and celebrate each little victory along the way.
- Be clear about why you want to break the habit and what you hope to achieve. Having specific goals can keep you motivated and focused on making positive changes.

- Make it easier to break your habit by changing your environment. Remove temptations or triggers from your surroundings and create a supportive environment that encourages your new habits.
- Share your goals with friends or family members who can support you on your journey. Having someone to hold you accountable can make all the difference.
- Breaking a habit takes time, so be patient with yourself. It is okay to slip up now and then – what is important is that you keep moving forward and do not give up.
- Celebrate your progress and reward yourself for your hard work. Treat yourself to something you enjoy whenever you reach a milestone or make significant strides in breaking your habit.

You will be surprised to know that it takes 21 days to form a habit and 90 days to make it a permanent lifestyle change.

But that first step is the toughest. I know because I have faced it.

When I was overcoming depression, I gained an extra 20 kg, reaching a weight of around 79 kg. As an author, blogger and what people often call a 'social media influencer', I needed to do shoots for brand collaborations, campaigns and event appearances.

Frankly, I disliked how I looked in my own photos and videos. I started turning down shoot offers because I knew it would make me feel bad about myself. But I was also aware that this was not the right solution. It was merely a temporary escape. Being in front of the camera is an integral part of my profession. This is how I pay my bills and put food on the table. The real solution was to stop being lazy and get back in shape.

Initially, I tried going for morning jogs but gave up after three days. Next, I attempted to do bollycardio at home by watching some YouTube videos, but that was a complete failure. No one was around to guide me, so I struggled to know whether I was doing it right or wrong.

I knew I had to hit the gym, but the idea of going felt like too much effort. I had settled into a comfortable routine: I woke up between 8:30 and 9:30 in the morning, went through my morning rituals, worked until lunchtime, took a lunch break, resumed work till 4:30 or 5 PM, took a power nap and then spent the evening with my family or engaged in hobbies. After dinner, I often returned to work or watched movies. It felt like I did not have time for anything else, and I thought I could not manage going to the gym. The first step seemed daunting. So what did I do?

My brother suggested that I go to the gym without overthinking it – just sign up for a six-month membership and pay with my debit card. He said that once my money was stuck, I would make sure to go, whether I felt like it or not. I decided to take his advice and signed up for a membership at a rather expensive gym in my area. Once I had done that, I had no choice but to go. Within a month, I started noticing changes in both my physical and mental health, and that was when I began to look forward to my gym sessions. In a few months, people started complimenting me, and I felt back on track – doing shoots and going to events.

I am truly grateful to my brother for that advice. It changed my life and revived me.

It may not be the same for you, but you need to figure out how to take that first step yourself.

For me, it all started when my money got tied up in a six-month gym membership. Coming from a humble background, spending ₹50,000 all at once was a significant commitment for me. After the membership expired, I did not renew it at the same gym. Instead, I found a gym and fitness studio near my home that was equally outstanding but offered more options, like yoga, aerobics and bollycardio, all at a much lower cost. By that point, going to the gym had become a habit. I realised that I did not need to tie up my money to motivate myself to work out; it was my own will that drove me to do it.

So how can you achieve this?

- **Identify your trigger**: For me, it was my money getting stuck. Your triggers can vary; they might be cues, rewards or consequences. (Not like punishing yourself physically, but more like setting a condition – if you complete a task, you can watch your favourite web series.) I often use this method when I am working on a book. As a huge movie buff, I set a goal for a specific word count, and I only allow myself to watch the next episode once I reach that goal.
- **Start small**: This always helps. Breaking a habit can be made easier by dividing it into the smallest possible steps. Focus on taking one tiny action at a time. For example, if your goal is to start exercising regularly, begin by committing to just five minutes of activity each day.
- **Keep it easy at first**: Make your new habit as easy and accessible as possible. Remove any barriers or obstacles that could prevent you from taking that first step. For example, if you want to start meditating, set a timer for just five minutes and find a quiet spot to sit.
- **Create a plan**: Develop a detailed plan for implementing your new habit. Write down exactly what you will do, when you will do it and how you will overcome any challenges that may arise. Having this plan in place will help you feel more prepared and confident when taking that first step.
- **Look forward**: Remind yourself of the benefits you will gain by adopting this new habit. Visualise how your life will improve and how you will feel once you have successfully integrated this habit into your routine. Keeping these positive outcomes in mind can help motivate you to take that initial leap.

Remember, the first step is just that – the first step.

It does not have to be perfect or monumental. The important thing is to take action and start moving towards your goals. Once you have overcome that initial hurdle, each subsequent step will become a little easier, and before you know it, your new habit will feel like a natural part of your routine.

Just keep reminding yourself that when you feel the urge to quit, you have got this and you can do it.

Prompts for Building Healthy Habits

Take a journal and write the answers to these questions:
- What is my bad habit?
- What is the solution to this?
- If I replace this habit with something, what are my options?
- Why am I not taking the step?
- What will I gain if I quit this bad habit?
- What is a new healthy habit that I need to build?
- Why do I need to build this habit?
- What is the first step towards it?
- What are its benefits?
- Did I take the first step today?

18

Manifest

IMAGINE A LIFE WHERE you can focus on what truly matters to you, you are aligned with your goals, and you can manifest every single thing you desire: money, health, relationships, assets, travel and more.

What if I told you this could actually happen? What if I spilled the secret about manifesting anything you want? It would be amazing, would it not?

The real purpose of shooing away the noises is to be able to focus on your goals and fulfil all your dreams and desires. It becomes meaningless if you successfully eliminate all noises and barriers from your life but have no actual intention, goal or higher purpose behind it.

This is why, in this final segment of the book, we will discuss how to manifest the next step after you successfully shoo the noises away.

What if I said you could manifest anything you want?

I am not even kidding. This is possible. We humans can manifest anything we want by practising manifestation.

Manifestation is not some magic or witchcraft. It is a science-based technique. It is completely logical and technical.

Neuroscience studies have revealed that when we engage in mental imagery, our brains light up similarly to how they would if we were experiencing those scenarios in real life. This suggests that by visualising our goals, we are priming our minds to view them as achievable and concrete, thus making it simpler to pursue them actively. Remember the example I gave you of a red car? You plan to buy a red car and suddenly start seeing red cars everywhere.

We have already discussed how the brain functions and the basics of neuroplasticity, which is responsible for manifesting things. Obviously, we will not discuss the same thing again, but here, we will explore some practical tips to help you manifest anything you want.

So what exactly is manifestation?

Manifestation is the process of bringing something into reality through your thoughts, beliefs, feelings and actions. It is based on the idea that our thoughts and emotions can influence the world around us, shaping our experiences and outcomes. Manifestation involves focusing your energy and attention on a specific desire or goal, believing in its attainment and taking inspired action to bring it to fruition.

The concept of manifestation is rooted in various spiritual and metaphysical beliefs, including the law of attraction, which suggests that like attracts like. According to this principle, maintaining positive thoughts and feelings can attract positive experiences and outcomes.

Manifestation is not just about wishing for something to happen and sitting back passively. It requires active participation and alignment with your desires on both conscious and subconscious levels. This may involve visualisation, affirmations, setting clear intentions and taking inspired action towards your goals.

Manifestation is tapping into your own inner power to create the life you want and deserve. It is about becoming aware of your thoughts and beliefs, cultivating a positive mindset and consciously co-creating your reality.

I am a Hindu who grew up in a spiritual and religious environment.

In Hindu mythology, the concept of manifestation is deeply intertwined with the belief in the power of intention and the divine creative force. The principle of manifestation is reflected in various Hindu scriptures, stories and spiritual practices.

One of the central ideas in Hinduism is that the universe is created, sustained and eventually dissolved by the divine energy known as Brahman. Brahman is considered the ultimate reality, and all of existence is seen as a manifestation of Brahman's divine energy.

The process of manifestation is depicted through various epics in Hindu mythology. For example, 'sankalpa' refers to the power of intention or resolve. The universe was believed to have been created when Brahman had the sankalpa or intention to manifest itself into the material world. This act of divine intention set the cosmic cycle of creation, preservation and dissolution into motion.

Hindu mythology is also rich with stories of gods and goddesses who manifest themselves in various forms to fulfil specific purposes or to guide and protect humanity. For instance, Lord Vishnu, one of the principal deities in Hinduism, is known for his avatars or incarnations, where he manifests in different forms to restore cosmic order and protect dharma (righteousness).

Moreover, yoga and meditation in Hinduism are often aimed at harnessing the power of manifestation. Through techniques such as visualisation, concentration and mantra repetition, practitioners seek to align their consciousness with the divine creative energy within themselves and the universe.

Let us understand the concept of sankalpa in a bit more depth because when manifesting anything, intention is everything.

Think of sankalpa as making a firm decision or resolution to achieve something meaningful to you.

When you have a strong sankalpa, it is like planting a seed of intention in the fertile soil of your consciousness. This intention acts as a guiding force, directing your thoughts, actions and energy towards your desired outcome.

The idea behind sankalpa is that when you set a clear and positive intention, you align yourself with the creative energy of the universe. It is like sending out a signal to the cosmos about what you want to manifest in your life.

But here's the key: Sankalpa is not just about wishing for something to happen and then sitting back. It is about committing yourself wholeheartedly to your goal and being willing to put in the effort and take action to make it happen.

As I said, intention is everything.

Intention is the first step of manifestation. You must be precise when setting an intention before you begin manifesting.

You need to tell your brain exactly what you want. Vague ideas, vague goals and vague concepts will only bring you distracted energy.

Suppose you say, 'I want to become successful in life', and this is your intention. In one of the previous chapters, I explained that too many forms of success exist. And you do not even know what thoughts are sitting in your subconscious mind. So when you start to work towards this intention, it will bring you so many back-and-forth energies, making you feel like you are progressing, but it is not what you wanted. So what needs to be done?

Be clear.

I want to become the CEO of this company in the next one year. I want to get a 15 LPA or above job. I want to be admitted to Harvard University for a BA in Fine Arts in 2025. I want a #1 bestseller on Amazon for my current book. I want to make ₹5,000 in sales every day. I want to get married to John Doe in December. I want to lose 15 kg in two months.

These are examples of clear intentions.

But when you are practising any manifestation technique, this is not how you should be putting it out.

For the universe, divine energies or even your brain, time is defined by your perception.

This means that there is no past or future; everything exists in the present moment. When you adopt this mindset – believing that you have what you desire now – you start to attract more of it into your life.

This is where affirmations come into play!

I have shared many affirmations in this book because my intention was to help you cultivate a positive mindset while you read and learn.

You can achieve what you affirm but that affirmation must be 100 per cent accepted by your energy system and your brain.

See, I firmly believe in the 12 laws of the universe. Here, in this segment, I will specifically talk about the law of attraction because we are discussing manifestation, and this law is everything you need to know when trying to manifest.

The law of attraction is one of the most well-known laws of the universe, followed by people all over the world. It simply means you attract what you focus on. If you focus on good, you attract more of it. If you focus on negativity, you attract more of it.

As simple as it sounds, it requires a lot of effort.

As I have explained previously, our brains are wired to pay attention to things that match our beliefs and expectations. This is called confirmation bias, right?

But it is not just about thinking happy thoughts and waiting for magic to happen. The law of attraction requires action too. You cannot just sit back and expect the universe, divine energy, gods or angels to do all the heavy lifting.

You have to take inspired action, put in the effort and make things happen.

And that is where it gets tough for some people. Because let us face it, change is hard. Stepping out of your comfort zone, facing your fears and putting in the work – it is not always rainbows and sunshine. Throughout this book, I have explained how to eliminate negativity from your life to gain a clear vision of the future.

Most people fail to manifest their desires because consciously, they are indeed waiting for things to happen, being all positive, trying to shoo away the noises, but deep down, doubts or fears hold them back. It is like having one foot on the accelerator and the other on the brake – you are not going anywhere fast.

When it works for someone, they start to believe in it firmly but when it does not give the desired results, people dismiss it.

If I talk about myself, I 100 per cent believe in the powers of the universe and its laws.

You see, everything is energy. Whatever you can see, touch, sense, feel, smell or hear is energy; even this book you are holding right now is energy.

And if we talk about the universe, it has infinite energy.

From a scientific point of view, the universe is indeed vast and seemingly boundless. According to modern physics, energy cannot be created or destroyed; it can only change forms. This principle, known as the conservation of energy, implies that the total energy within a closed system like the universe remains constant over time. So in that sense, the universe does possess an immense amount of energy.

Even theories like the Big Bang suggest that the universe underwent a rapid expansion from a highly compressed state, releasing enormous amounts of energy in the process. This energy continues to shape the universe's evolution, driving the motion of celestial bodies, the formation of stars and galaxies, and the fundamental interactions between particles.

On a philosophical or metaphysical level, some people interpret the idea of infinite energy in a more abstract or spiritual sense. They might view the universe as an interconnected web of energy, where everything exists in various forms – matter, light, sound, thoughts, emotions and so on. In this view, the universe's energy is not limited by physical boundaries but flows endlessly throughout existence.

I personally believe our brain is the real hero here.

Indeed, everything we talked about earlier is 100 per cent true but if the brain does not allow all this to get into your system and work on it, it is useless.

When we utilise the energy of the universe and use our brains in the correct way that is when we start to manifest our desires.

There are some brilliant manifestation techniques that have helped billions of people around the world, including myself, manifest successfully.

There is no 'more effective' or 'less effective' in these techniques. Whatever practical manifestation techniques I will share now work brilliantly because all of them are based on one common rule – consistency.

Consistency is the ultimate key for practising manifestation – and in life in general.

You may have often heard people arguing about which is the most effective way to lose weight. Some say yoga does not work, some say Zumba is the best way, some swear by the gym, while others claim they lost weight by simply walking. There is no right or wrong here. The key is consistency. If you do any activity consistently, you will start to notice positive results.

The same is true for manifestation techniques. If you practise them consistently, they will work for you.

And yes, do not worry if you are unable to follow everything at once, just take baby steps and start with one or two techniques.

Affirmations

Let us begin with my favourite manifestation technique – affirmation. Now, I have already explained several times what affirmations are and the easiest way to work with them is by writing them or chanting them. Here is exactly how you can start working with affirmations:

Write

I love this one. Every day, write one page of affirmations. You can either repeat the same affirmation multiple times, such as: 'I am a money magnet. I am a money magnet. I am a money magnet.' Or you can write different affirmations like: 'I am a money magnet. I attract money easily. I live in abundance. Money is my best friend.'

Here is what I like to do:
- If I am trying to manifest something specific, I write the same affirmation on the entire page.

- On regular days, I write a list of different affirmations.

Chant

Chanting is one of the best ways to manifest anything. Chanting affirmations is easy and can be done at any time. There are no strict rules for chanting affirmations. You can do it at any time of the day or night and anywhere. If you chant in front of a mirror, it can yield miraculous results.

Listen

Listening to affirmations is effective too. You can simply record your personal affirmation using the voice recorder on your phone and listen to it. Otherwise, use YouTube to listen to affirmations; it has many free videos. Now let us understand how to create a perfect affirmation that works wonders for you.

The first thing you should do is identify what your intention or goal is. You need to clearly define what you want to manifest in your life. Whether it is improved confidence, financial abundance, better health or fulfilling relationships, be specific about your desired outcome.

Then, write your affirmation as if your goal has already been achieved. This helps shift your mindset and beliefs towards your desired reality. For example, instead of saying, 'I will be successful,' say, 'I am successful.'

Remember, phrases like 'I want', 'I need', 'I desire' and 'I am longing for' signal to your brain that you lack these things in your life, reinforcing a sense of absence, which means you are focusing on the negative.

So frame your affirmation in positive terms, focusing on what you want rather than what you do not want. For instance, say. 'I am attracting prosperity' instead of 'I am not broke' or 'I live in abundance' instead of 'I am worthy of abundance'.

You also need to tailor your affirmation to reflect your own experiences and desires. Use 'I' statements to make it more personal and empowering. This helps establish a deeper connection with the affirmation. For example, say, 'I am loved and respected' instead of 'People love and respect me'.

It is important to keep your affirmation concise and to the point. Yes, the shorter, the crisper, the better. This makes it easier to remember and repeat regularly. Focus on one specific aspect of your goal rather than trying to cover too much ground in one affirmation. For example, instead of saying, 'I am a money magnet, I radiate love and I attract all the happiness in life where people respect me', you can break it down into smaller sentences like 'I am a money magnet', 'I radiate love', 'I am treated with respect and love by others' and 'I am attracting all the happiness in life'.

It does not matter how many affirmations you use in one go; the idea is to feed the brain with small yet powerful morsels rather than long confusing statements that even you cannot remember.

Another important aspect is to include emotional language in your affirmation to evoke the feelings associated with achieving your goal. This helps align your thoughts and emotions with your desired outcome. For instance, say, 'I am overflowing with gratitude for my abundance' instead of 'I have money' (although 'I have money' is also a good affirmation, it will have a limited impact).

Vision Board

A vision board is not just a tool to gain a clear vision of your future and practise mindfulness; it is also a powerful technique for manifestation.

You see, everything is interconnected. Once you have a clear vision of the future, you will be able to focus more on it.

Suppose you want to manifest a white bungalow with a lush green garden and a swimming pool. You find an exact picture and put it on your vision board.

Now, what happens? First, you gain a clear vision of exactly how you want your dream house to be. Second, your brain will start working towards manifesting it. You will start to see opportunities and circumstances that help you manifest it.

Vision boards are closely aligned with the principles of the law of attraction. According to this universal law, like attracts like, and by focusing on positive thoughts and emotions, you attract corresponding experiences into your life.

Vision boards serve as visual affirmations of your desires, helping shift your vibrational frequency to match the frequency of your goals.

Vision boards tap into the power of the subconscious mind. When you regularly view your vision board, especially during relaxed or meditative states, you bypass the conscious mind's filters and directly influence your subconscious beliefs. This alignment between your conscious desires and subconscious beliefs is crucial for manifestation.

So how do you work with vision boards to manifest anything?

- Place your vision board where you can see it multiple times a day, such as near your dressing mirror, at your work desk, beside your bedside table, in your cupboard or even within your daily planner.
- Set aside at least five minutes each day to gaze at your vision board. Try to immerse yourself in the feelings you will experience when you manifest those goals, almost like daydreaming. During other times of the day, a quick glance at the board – whether consciously or subconsciously – can still be effective.
- Make your vision board as visually attractive as possible so that it genuinely brings you joy.

Watch or Read Success Stories

Do a small test on yourself. Listen to a fictional story about how a person became a millionaire after being born poor, and then listen to a real-life experience of someone going from rags to riches. What will inspire and motivate you more? Of course, the real-life story.

When we see real-life examples of someone making their dreams a reality, it always has a profound impact on our own beliefs and aspirations. Real-life success stories provide tangible proof that achieving our dreams is possible. When we read or watch stories about individuals who have overcome obstacles and achieved extraordinary success, it demonstrates that similar outcomes are within our reach. This tangible proof helps dissolve doubts and limiting beliefs, making our goals seem more attainable.

The best way to do this is to read inspiring non-fiction books like autobiographies of successful people or watch interviews. Although interviews are good for bite-sized motivation, books provide more details about a person's life journey. They cover every single experience – good, bad and ugly – including how they coped when life hit rock bottom, their struggles, their triumphs and so much more.

When we read about someone who has achieved success in a field or pursuit that resonates with us, we can easily identify with their journey. This sense of identification fosters the belief that if they can do it, so can we.

Real-life success stories offer valuable insights and lessons that we can apply to our own lives. By studying the strategies, mindset and actions of successful individuals, we gain practical knowledge and guidance for pursuing our own dreams. Just like the many personal experiences I have shared including the lessons and techniques that have helped me in my journey so far, I am sure you will try at least 5 per cent of my suggestions.

Learning from others' experiences can help us navigate challenges more effectively and make informed decisions on our path to success.

The achievements of others can ignite a fire within us, fuelling our motivation and determination to pursue our own goals. Their stories inspire us to dream bigger, work harder and never give up, even in the face of adversity. This inspiration serves as a powerful driving force that propels us forward on our journey towards manifesting our dreams.

Exposure to real-life success stories expands our belief system and shifts our perspective on what is possible. It challenges our preconceived notions of limitations and opens our minds to new possibilities and opportunities. As our belief in ourselves and our potential grows, so does our capacity to manifest our dreams.

So pick an inspiring autobiography of a successful person. As you are reading this book, I assume you like reading. However, if you do not enjoy reading books, you can also listen to audiobooks. They are equally effective.

Now, how do you incorporate this into your manifestation process?

Let me explain with an example. Suppose you aspire to become a cricketer. Start by reading autobiographies of successful cricketers like Sachin Tendulkar and Ricky Ponting.

After reading these books, find ways to make them relatable. Also, note down the techniques and tips they used to overcome setbacks and difficult situations.

While reading or listening, remind yourself that this person, too, was once an ordinary person like you and has succeeded in achieving their dream. Visualise yourself achieving everything that you desire throughout the process; it truly works wonders.

Play 'As If'

Have you ever played 'teacher-teacher' or 'doctor-doctor' with your cousins or friends? Well, I want you to play 'as if' with yourself.

'As if' is a simple game that you can play alone at least once a day, even if it is for five minutes. There are no specific rules for this game; all you need to do is pretend 'as if' you have already achieved what you desire. Act and behave 'as if' your desired outcome has already manifested in your life.

Suppose you want to win an award at your office. Play 'as if' you have already won the award, practise the speech that you will give when you receive it and pretend to say thank you when everyone congratulates you. It is more like 'fake it till you make it' but when you are alone.

I am sure you now have an idea of what playing 'as if' is all about.

If your goal is to become a successful entrepreneur, think and believe like a successful entrepreneur. Replace doubts and limiting beliefs with confidence and positivity.

Visualise yourself already living the reality of your desired outcome. Imagine the details of what your life looks, feels and sounds like once your goal is achieved.

Engage all your senses in the visualisation to make it as vivid and real as possible. By immersing yourself in this mental imagery, you send a powerful message to your subconscious mind and the universe about what you want to manifest.

Embody the emotions associated with achieving your goal. Whether it is joy, excitement, gratitude or fulfilment, allow yourself to feel those emotions as if your goal has already come to fruition. Emotions are powerful energy amplifiers and can magnetise your desires to you more quickly.

Practise gratitude for your desired outcome as if it has already happened. Express appreciation for the blessings, opportunities and experiences that come with manifesting your goal. By cultivating an attitude of gratitude, you raise your vibration and attract more of what you are grateful for into your life.

The most important thing is to have fun, release any resistance or doubt and surrender to the flow of life. When we start to feel pressure or tension about something, we create resistance in our manifestation.

It is simple: if you keep thinking that money is hard to get, then money will indeed be hard to acquire. However, the moment you shift to a mindset of ease, you will find that manifesting money becomes effortless – this is where the magic begins.

Raise Your Vibrations

You must have heard the famous phrase – Good vibes only.

What does this mean? It means good vibrations only.

Everything in the universe has a vibration, including thoughts, emotions and physical matter and each vibrates at a different frequency.

This concept is rooted in quantum physics and metaphysical principles. Every object, person and even abstract concepts like thoughts and emotions emit energy vibrations that can be measured.

As humans, our thoughts, emotions and beliefs also emit energetic vibrations, and we are constantly oscillating at different frequencies depending on our internal state. When we feel positive emotions like love, joy and gratitude, we vibrate at a higher frequency. On the other hand, when we experience negative emotions like fear, anger or sadness, our vibration becomes lower.

The idea is that by consciously raising our vibrations – through positive thoughts, emotions and actions – we can align ourselves with higher frequencies and attract more positive experiences into our lives. This is a fundamental principle in manifestation and the law of attraction. So by elevating our vibrations, we can manifest our desires and create a more fulfilling reality.

Low-vibrational frequencies include feelings of fear, anger, hatred, jealousy, guilt, shame, resentment, doubt, despair and self-criticism. High-vibrational frequencies include feelings of gratitude, love, peace, joy, compassion, forgiveness, optimism, empowerment, creativity and abundance.

So every 'noise' that we discussed in this book causes us to be in a low-vibrational frequency. It acts as a barrier to manifestation and hence, we need to switch from a low-vibrational frequency to a higher one in order to manifest anything. This is what raising your vibrations means!

One's vibrations can be increased in many ways.

Some of the methods we have already discussed include practising gratitude, being mindful, meditating, surrounding ourselves with positivity, engaging in self-care, listening to uplifting music, performing acts of kindness, visualisations, using affirmations, healing, etc.

But there are more ways to raise our vibrations.

One of the best ways is to have crystals around you.

Crystals are believed to emit vibrations at a consistent frequency due to their atomic structure. When we come into contact with crystals, their vibrations can influence and harmonise with our own energetic field, helping to raise our vibrations to a higher level.

Crystals are commonly used in healing modalities such as Reiki. Many Reiki practitioners, including myself, incorporate crystals during their sessions to balance energies, clear spiritual blocks and release mental and emotional blockages. Crystals may be placed directly on the body, arranged around it or held in the practitioner's hands.

Research has shown that crystals carry energy and possess high vibrations.

It is essential to know which type of crystal is suitable for your needs. For instance, if you want to manifest money, pyrite or citrine can be beneficial. If you are healing from an emotional wound, amethyst will help you, while rose quartz is ideal for attracting love into your life.

So how can you effectively work with crystals?

If you search on Google about working with crystals, you will find thousands of methods.

I believe there are no strict rules when it comes to using crystals. You can use them however you like. For instance, you can carry a crystal in your pocket, place it on your work desk or in the living room, or wear it as jewellery. Personally, I have raw crystal stones scattered throughout my house, but I enjoy wearing crystal bracelets.

The key thing to remember is that crystals only work when you charge them with your intentions.

If you buy a crystal and simply place it on your desk or wear it as a bracelet, thinking it will magically work for you, it will not be effective. While it will emit energies, those energies might not align with what you want. It is similar to asking an assistant to complete tasks without providing clear instructions – they will not know what to do without a proper to-do list.

So how do you put intentions into your crystals?

The simplest way is to hold your crystal between both of your palms and state your intention (affirmation) of what you want to manifest. Do not count; just repeat it a few times until you can focus clearly and then place the crystal where you would like or wear it.

Another important thing to note is that crystals carry energy, so it is important to cleanse them once you purchase them. You can cleanse your crystals using an incense stick or by washing them. I personally prefer using water from the River Ganga to wash gemstones and crystals, but you can use any river or fresh water for this purpose.

Affirmations to Raise Your Vibrations and Manifest

- I am attracting all the good things that life has to offer.
- I attract abundance and prosperity into my life effortlessly.
- I attract opportunities that align with my highest good.
- I am confident.
- Every day, I am becoming the best version of myself.
- I radiate love, joy and positivity, and I attract the same energy into my life.
- I trust in the divine timing of the universe, and everything is unfolding perfectly for me.
- I am grateful for the abundance that flows into my life in expected and unexpected ways.
- I am a magnet for success.
- I am perfectly aligned with the energy of abundance.
- I co-create my destiny.
- I manifest anything I want.

Inspiring Quotes

Believe you can and you are halfway there.
> - Theodore Roosevelt

Imagination is everything. It is the preview of life's coming attractions.
> - Albert Einstein

What you think, you become. What you feel, you attract. What you imagine, you create.
> - Buddha

You are the master of your destiny. You can influence, direct and control your own environment. You can make your life what you want it to be.
> - Napoleon Hill

Whatever the mind can conceive and believe, it can achieve.
> - Napoleon Hill

19

Embrace the Noise-Free Life

YOU MADE IT TO the final chapter of this book. Before I begin, I want to thank you from the bottom of my heart and soul. You have given me a morsel of the most important and valuable asset of your life, for which I am eternally grateful. I will tell you what it is in a bit.

So we have talked about noises, their kinds, their cost, our brains, success, resilience, mindfulness, self-worth, our limits and everything needed to elevate our lives. In this final chapter, I want to talk about the biggest and most valuable asset that connects and binds everything we have discussed so far – time.

Yes, time is our biggest and most valuable asset.

We often think we have time, that we can do it tomorrow or next week, but we do not realise that today is the most important day of our lives. Why? Because it is never going to come back.

To succeed in life, you need to start valuing time – yours and others'.

The person who does not value time fails big time!

Think about it for a moment. Each day, we are given the same 24 hours to work with. It is the one thing we all have in common, regardless of our background, status or circumstances. And, despite its universal nature, time is something we often take for granted.

You see, time is unlike any other resource. It is not something we can earn more of or buy more of. Once it is gone, it is gone forever. That is why it is important to make the most of our time, cherish each moment and use it wisely.

Why is time our biggest asset?

It is because time is the one thing that can never be replaced.

No amount of money or success can buy us more time. It is a finite resource, and how we spend it is entirely up to us.

Think about the people who have inspired you throughout history. From leaders and visionaries to artists and innovators, they all had one thing in common: they understood the value of time. They did not waste a single moment; instead, they used their time to pursue their passions, make a difference in the world and leave a lasting legacy.

Take Steve Jobs, for example. He once said, 'Your time is limited; do not waste it living someone else's life.' Jobs understood that time was his most valuable asset, and he used it to build one of the most successful companies in the world – Apple Inc. He did not let the noises hold him back; instead, he embraced each moment as an opportunity to create something truly remarkable.

But it is not just famous figures who understand the value of time. Each and every one of us has the power to make the most of the time we have been given. Whether pursuing our dreams, spending time with loved ones or simply enjoying the beauty of the world, every moment is an opportunity to create something meaningful and memorable.

Yes, time is priceless.

And the worst part is that you do not know what happens next. I realised this the hard way. I had planned to surprise my parents with something they had always asked me for. I delayed it just because I thought I would do it in a certain year, in a certain way. But I could not do it. Both of my parents departed forever, leaving a heavy regret in my heart.

I do not want you to learn the value of time this way. Understand this – time is precious. Every single second is precious.

Ask about the importance of one minute from those who missed a train. Ask about the importance of one second, from someone who just avoided an accident. Ask about the importance of one millisecond, from an athlete who won a silver medal in the Olympics but lost the gold.

It is high time we made the most of our time. Only then will all our efforts to shoo the noises reap the best benefits.

So how can we make the most of our time?

It all starts with awareness. We must be mindful of how we spend our time and whether it aligns with our values and goals. Are we investing our time in things that truly matter to us or are we squandering it on distractions and trivialities?

Setting goals and priorities is one way to make the most of our time. By identifying what is most important to us and focusing our time and energy on those things, we can ensure that we progress towards our dreams and aspirations. Whether starting a new business, pursuing a passion project or strengthening our relationships, setting clear goals can help us stay focused and motivated.

But it is not just about setting goals, it is also about taking action.

As the saying goes, 'Don't watch the clock; do what it does. Keep going.'

We must be willing to take bold and decisive action in pursuit of our goals, even when the path ahead seems uncertain or challenging. Time waits for no one, and if we want to make the most of it, we must be willing to seize the moment and make things happen.

But what exactly is a noise-free life?

A noise-free life is about breaking barriers, eliminating blockages and setting yourself free from limits to become unstoppable. It is about showing the world that you are made of stardust. Though we are all made of stardust, only a handful of us shine.

Everyone has a goal, whether personal or professional. We all want to be successful. But know that success is a journey, not a destination. And when you start this journey, you need to be consistent.

You see, consistency is the key to unlocking the door to success.

Imagine you wish to learn to play the guitar. If you practise for a few hours one day and then stop for weeks, you will not make much progress.

Consistency transforms ordinary actions into extraordinary results. It is about showing up daily, even when you do not feel like it, even when the going gets tough. It is about committing to yourself and sticking to it, no matter what.

Athletes do not become champions by training sporadically; they do it by putting in the work every day, rain or shine. Writers do not finish novels by writing only when inspiration strikes; they do it by sitting at their desks and putting pen to paper, even on days when the words do not flow. It happens to me a lot – I often find myself sitting and staring at my diary or laptop for hours, but I show up; even if I write just two sentences, I show up consistently.

Even when trying to lose weight, no matter the method, yoga, gym, jogging, running or dancing, you will only succeed if you are consistent.

Consistency builds momentum. It is like pushing a boulder up a hill; it might feel slow and steady at first, but as you keep going, you start to pick up speed. Before you know it, you have reached the top.

But know that consistency is not just about brute force or sheer willpower. It is also about creating habits and routines that support your goals. It is about setting yourself up for success by making small, sustainable changes that add up over time.

So whether you are chasing your dreams, working towards a goal or simply trying to be the best version of yourself, remember – consistency is your secret weapon. It is the magic ingredient that turns dreams into reality and aspirations into achievements.

May you win your battles. May you heal from the wounds that you hide from the world. May you find your mental noise-cancelling headphones that allow you to hear your own inner voice clearly and stop the noises blocking your way to success, happiness and abundance.

Stay blessed and keep thriving!

About the Author

Anamika Mishra is a certified life coach and travel blogger whose work inspires thousands to transform their lives. As a multi-genre writer, she delves into the intricacies of human relationships and personal growth, while her blog brings to life the magic of travel and self-discovery. A passionate traveller, she is also a popular travel influencer in India with more than a million fan following across social media platforms.

Anamika is the founder of Responsible Yatri, a digital platform promoting mindful and sustainable travel. A nature enthusiast and climate activist, she encourages travellers to explore responsibly, respect local cultures and reduce their environmental footprint.

Blending storytelling with actionable strategies, Anamika specialises in mindset mastery, emotional healing and the art of manifestation. Her books and blogs provide profound insights for creating balance, resilience and fulfilment along with her personal experiences about travel and life.